JESUS
ENCOUNTER

JESUS
ENCOUNTER

a personal guidebook

CAROLYN MOORE
with Kris Key

seedbed
PUBLISHING

Sowing for a Great Awakening

Library of Congress Control Number: 2013931012
Paperback ISBN: 978-1-62824-021-4
Mobipocket ISBN: 978-1-62824-044-3
ePub ISBN: 978-1-62824-045-0
uPDF ISBN: 978-1-62824-046-7

Cover and page design by Ellen Parker Bibb

SEEDBED PUBLISHING
204 N. Lexington Avenue
Wilmore, Kentucky 40390
www.seedbed.com

For Leroy,
who helped me encounter Jesus
at Maxwell House

CONTENTS

CONTENTS

HOW TO USE THIS BOOK

For this Encounter, you will need:

- A Bible
- A journal
- A couple of pens (in more than one color)
- An internet connection
- A quiet place where you can encounter Jesus

A note about how to use these resources

We want you to encounter Jesus. We've structured this guidebook with that encounter in mind. Rather than providing all the Scripture references within the text here, we are asking you to do the work of finding the passages in your own Bible, so you can mark up the sections studied and begin to create a habit of looking for where God is at work in Scripture. Sometimes we'll ask you to go online to find the lyrics of a song or to listen in on one we've found to be relevant. Though we do provide space to answer some questions directly in this book, for the most part we want you to write your responses in your own journal or notebook. By giving you resources and inviting your active participation, we hope to help you cultivate devotional practices that will continue long after this guidebook has been shelved.

A note from Carolyn about journaling

I have a confession to make. I've journaled on and off for years and, for the most part, it has been a richly rewarding part of my personal time with God. For way too long, however, my journal entries were written as if to be read. (Who knows? Maybe even published!) Because I approached journaling as if someone might one day read what I'd written, it always had a veneer to it. A little too much polish, not enough transparency.

I've since conquered that silliness and have learned how to write in my journal just for Jesus and me. I've discovered Jesus doesn't grade on penmanship. In my conversations with Him, I can be as messy as I want to be. I can scribble, cross through, make notes in the margins, draw nonsensical pictures, and generally do whatever works in the moment.

I often journal in two colors, writing my own thoughts in black or blue ink, and what I sense may be Spirit-inspired thoughts in red. When I come across a thought that seems profound ("smarter than I could have thought of myself," as Asbury professor Dr. Bob Tuttle would say), I note that thought in red, just like the words of Jesus in my Bible.

Sometimes I'll even write a question for Jesus at the top of the page, then journal everything I hear in red. I don't try to analyze it; I just listen and write. A week or so down the road, I may come back to that entry to see how it sounds with the benefit of a little time and perspective. Often, I am amazed at how helpful those entries can be to my journey with Jesus. I do believe He still speaks into our lives. I have encountered Him in the practice of journaling. I hope you will too.

In fact, I hope the combination of this guidebook, your own journal (or blog), the creative prayer exercises, interaction with the Word of God, and a quiet place to encounter Jesus will all converge to create a spiritual revival in your life.

Know that as you begin, I am praying for you.

INTRODUCTION

You are a rebel. I am a rebel. It is our nature to rebel. This is the human story. It began in Genesis with a loving God who invested all creatures with the power of choice. Before humans ever hit the scene, an angel in pursuit of the power of God rebelled against the holy order of things. It was not enough for him to worship God. He wanted to be like God, so he began to compete for that power and became God's adversary. God rejected him and ever since, he has been fighting against God for control of the human race. So this is our human condition: we are caught up in this spiritual battle for control of our souls. It is like the undertow. We are trying to get to the shore, but there is this constant force pulling us away from the direction we know we should be moving. This is what Paul means when he says our battle is not against flesh and blood but against the rulers, authorities, and powers of the dark world and against the forces of evil in the spiritual realm (Eph. 6:12).

Knowing we could never defeat that force on our own, God came to our rescue and restored our power to overcome the enemy. Because we couldn't do it on our own, He sent Christ to rescue us from the futility of our sin and to restore us to God. And He did it not on our strength, but on His grace.

INTRODUCTION

Jesus came to fight our battles for us.

No one paints that picture better than David in Psalm 18: "He reached down from on high and took hold of me; he drew me out of deep waters. He rescued me from my powerful enemy, from my foes, who were too strong for me. . . . He brought me out into a spacious place; he rescued me because he delighted in me" (Ps. 18:16–19).

And our only responsibility—our right response in light of that incredible gift—is simply to believe it. When we respond by faith, we encounter for ourselves the very One who has power to overcome our spiritual enemy.

As you read the Word, think through the questions, write in your journal, form your own prayers, and experience the activities in this guide, may you encounter *the* Jesus . . . who changes *everything*.

JESUS
ENCOUNTER

WEEK 1: EXERCISE #1

Let's start with Jesus.

In Colossians 1:15–23, Paul introduces us to our majestically cosmic yet intimately personal redeemer, Jesus. This is a stunning and compelling description of Christ. Read this passage aloud, as if you were introducing Jesus to an audience:

The Son is the image of the invisible God, the firstborn over all creation. For in him all things were created: things in heaven and on earth, visible and invisible, whether thrones or powers or rulers or authorities; all things have been created through him and for him. He is before all things, and in him all things hold together. And he is the head of the body, the church; he is the beginning and the firstborn from among the dead, so that in everything he might have the supremacy. For God was pleased to have all his fullness dwell in him, and through him to reconcile to himself all things, whether things on earth or things in heaven, by making peace through his blood, shed on the cross. Once you were alienated from God and were enemies in your minds because of your evil behavior. But now he has reconciled you by Christ's physical body through death to present you holy in his sight, without blemish and free from accusation—if you continue in your faith, established and firm, and do not move from the hope held out in the gospel. This is the gospel that you heard and that has been proclaimed to every creature under heaven, and of which I, Paul, have become a servant.

Now take a pen or highlighter and highlight words or phrases that stand out. Better yet, mark it up in your Bible and not just here in this book. Square it or underline it or highlight any way you can to make it jump off the page. This is a text you will want to return to frequently and perhaps even commit to memory.

Now repeat this process with Hebrews 1:1–4. Read it silently from your Bible. Now read it aloud. Highlight, underline, and circle words and phrases that stand out for you.

Repeat the process once more with John 14:6–9.

What do these texts have in common?

How would you summarize the central idea they hold in common?

Encounter

Write this phrase on a pocket-sized card you can carry with you: "He is the image of the invisible God."

On the back write this: "He is the exact representation of His being."

Now spend time whispering these words to yourself. Do this throughout the day. Meditate on these lines as you invite the Spirit of God to "sow" them into your heart.

WEEK 1: EXERCISE #2

If we want to see God, we must start with Jesus. When we begin with a vague notion of what God is like we tend to project our own experiences, for better or worse, in formulating this image. ("Because my father was absent, God must be distant." "Because my childhood pastor stole from the church, God can't be trusted.") If we extrapolate our vision of Jesus from our faulty understanding of God, we don't wind up seeing the real Jesus. Sure, we might see *a* Jesus, but we will miss *the* Jesus. And let's face it: there are some very flawed images of Jesus out there.

In fact, to one degree or another we all have a distorted sense of God's image. It comes primarily from three sources: our parents, the church, and traumatic experiences. Obviously, not every influence is negative, but a little here and a little there and before we know it, we have missed a biblical understanding of God.

The aim of this study is to help us get a better, more biblical image of *the* Jesus we claim to follow. The way we understand God (in Jesus) largely determines the way we see ourselves. The way we see ourselves determines the way we treat others. Follow the logic? Our ability to accurately reflect the image of God depends on our vision of who God is and what God is like.

Take five minutes to read and reflect on the text below:

Follow God's example, therefore, as dearly loved children and walk in the way of love, just as Christ loved us and gave himself up for us as a fragrant offering and sacrifice to God.

—Ephesians 5:1–2

Encounter

Take a few minutes to sketch out in your journal examples of how your image of God has been shaped by parents, the church, or experience. If you can't come up with personal examples, make some observations of how you have seen this at play in others.

The secret to understanding who God is and consequently who we really are is to start with Jesus. The problem is that there are a lot of versions of Jesus out there. The only trustworthy way to understand Jesus is to study His Word with others *in the power of the Holy Spirit.* We must have a trustworthy, authoritative source. That source is the Bible, the inspired Word of God.

WEEK 1: EXERCISE #3

If we are created in the image of the invisible God and yet that image has been ruined by sin, we have a problem. God is invisible. How are we to see that which we are to become?

If Jesus is the visible representation of the invisible God we have a solution: our quest is to encounter this Jesus as revealed by Word and Spirit.

Read 2 Corinthians 3:12–4:6.

Make some observations about what you learn from this text.

What does Paul teach us here about encountering Jesus?

Make a note of any questions this text raises for you.

According to this text, what is the role of the Holy Spirit in leading us to encounter Jesus?

Encounter

Using a journal to record your thoughts and a highlighter to mark your Bible, read slowly through Isaiah 42:1–7. Mark any words or phrases you believe point to the coming Messiah. Meditate on those words you've highlighted. How do you encounter Jesus in this Old Testament passage? How does Isaiah describe the character of God's chosen One? Make a list of attributes.

Now, repeat this same exercise using Isaiah 53. How do you encounter Jesus in this passage? What do you learn about the character of God's Messiah?

In your journal, write a prayer of praise to Jesus that reflects what you've learned about Him in this encounter.

WEEK 1: EXERCISE #4

In our quest to encounter Jesus, we may gain the largest perspective by beginning with the end. This week's video teaching comes from Matthew's Gospel, where Jesus talks here about His second coming and the end of the age. Let's look together at some of the texts we'll encounter in the teaching session.

In Matthew 24:4–14, Jesus explains to His followers about the end of the age. Some call it "the end times," when Jesus will return to reign supreme. In this scene, it is two days before the Passover and Jesus has been teaching in the temple in Jerusalem. As He leaves the temple, He comments to His disciples that not one stone will be left on another and that "every one will be thrown down." They travel up to the Mount of Olives, about a mile from Jerusalem, and look out over the city. The disciples begin to ask Jesus specifically what will happen at the end of the age when He comes again.

As Jesus gazes out over the Holy City, His mission to fulfill His Father's purpose looms large. Jesus doesn't just see a city down below. When Jesus gazes down, He "sees" with God's perspective. He sees beyond the walls of the city and into the hearts of the people who live there. His perspective comes from the heart of the Father who sent Him on a mission to reach all nations. The end game? That *all* may come to encounter Him as Lord and Savior.

The disciples' perspective, on the other hand, is much different. They are all about the "when" and "how" of Jesus' second coming, not so much the impact of His message in the "here and now." They are more interested in knowing the facts than in living a Kingdom life.

Read Matthew 24:4–5.

The Greek word for "watch" in this passage is *blepo*. That word means to look at, to become aware of, observe and discern or perceive. In contrast, to "deceive" means to make a person believe that which is not true, to mislead them or lead them astray.

What do you think the disciples' perception was of the city of Jerusalem as they looked down from the Mount of Olives?

What does Jesus warn His disciples to watch out for?

Read Matthew 24:6–10.

Jesus tells His disciples not to be alarmed or troubled in verse 6. The Greek word here is *throeo*. It means to wail or be frightened. In verse 8, "birth pains" in the Greek is *odino*, which means that all the suffering, death, and destruction is only the beginning of pain and anguish.

After Jesus paints such a bleak picture of the future, how do you think the disciples felt?

What do you think ultimately kept the disciples from being alarmed and what kept them faithful to Jesus?

Read Matthew 24:11–14.

In verse 13, we read Jesus' instruction to stand firm to the end. "Standing firm" means to endure; to bear trials and have fortitude; to persevere and remain steadfast; to be faithful to the end.

How will the disciples stand firm during this impending time of wickedness and protect their hearts from growing cold?

What does Jesus tell the disciples will be the reward for standing firm? What will be the ultimate result of their faithfulness?

Encounter

In the traditional liturgy of the Eucharist, we proclaim the mystery of the faith: "Christ has died. Christ is risen. Christ will come again." We may not understand the universal impact of these words (they are a mystery, after all!), yet they are our hope. Christ has come, and Christ *will* come again!

Say these words aloud to yourself. "Christ has died. Christ is risen. Christ will come again." Write them as a heading in your journal, then reflect on what they mean for you. What emotions do they evoke?

Meditate on the picture of the second coming of the Messiah as it is painted for us by John in Revelation 19:11–16. What new images of Jesus do you discover in this passage? How does this picture of Jesus compare with the images you found in Isaiah?

In your journal, write a prayer of praise to Jesus inspired by what you learn about Him in Revelation 19.

WEEK 1: EXERCISE #5

Jesus wants His disciples to begin to see things as He sees them. He wants them to have the bigger picture, to have eyes to see and ears to hear what the Spirit is saying to the world.

It is the same for us. Jesus wants all who follow Him to see things from His perspective. That means not just getting facts, but having an authentic encounter with Jesus, the Christ. By studying His words, understanding His compassion for people, and grasping His eternal perspective, we can carry on the Kingdom business God entrusted to His Son.

Jesus' words in Matthew 24 are powerful and direct. He wants us to know Him in the deepest, most personal way. He wants us to watch out, be aware, and perceive those who would mislead us. He wants us to have the spiritual courage to remain faithful even when it is hard. When we trust His promise of deliverance and keep our perspective and priorities focused on Him, we will encounter the authentic Jesus.

Read Romans 10:12–15.

According to this passage, how is salvation achieved?

How would you put this passage in chart form—beginning with the gospel message and ending with the one who shares it?

How is *the* Jesus asking you to share the good news in your life?

Encounter

If there is one thing we've learned in life, it is that we human beings have an almost infinite capacity to deceive ourselves. It's why we desperately need the Word of God and the community of the church.

How do you recognize deception? Where in your life are you most likely to be led astray?

Have you had a saving encounter with Jesus Christ? Have you trusted Christ as your Savior? Are you ready to make that decision, or do you need more time to learn and consider it all?

What is your spiritual story? Write it down in a few paragraphs. Would you be willing to consider sharing that with your group?

In what ways do you think you reflect the image of Jesus Christ? In what ways do you think you *deflect* His image?

Do you really believe that Jesus Christ is coming again to judge the living and the dead? What questions do you have? What doubts?

Does Jesus' return evoke fear in you or hope or some mixture of the two? Describe that.

In tough times, what helps you to stay faithful? What practices keep you spiritually centered? What habits help to keep your heart "warm"?

What personal commitments will you make as a result of this study?

WEEK 2: EXERCISE #1

Jesus lived a prophetic life. He revealed God in His character, behavior, and teaching. In Jesus, we understand God's nature is to love, His salvation is based on grace, and His heart is for the whole world.

A prophet reveals where God is working to reconcile the world to Himself. They show us truths about God and ourselves we may not have seen on our own. Woven throughout the Old Testament are words, statements, and stories that point toward where God is at work and where He is headed. One such line is embedded in the book of Esther.

Read Esther 4.

In this prophetic word, Mordecai tells Esther she may well have been created for "just such a time as this." She is making her choice about how to respond to a dangerous situation, and God calls her (through Mordecai's word) to join Him where He is already at work. There is an overtone of trust in Mordecai's statement. Deliverance will come. God will redeem His people, if not now then eventually. Her response will determine her place in God's plan.

Mordecai offers sage wisdom. If Esther tries to save her own life, he warns, she'll lose it. If she does not take up the call, God will find someone else. In an act of unusual courage, Esther steps into obedience on the strength of Mordecai's word. She calls for the people to pray and fast, and then to watch for God's time.

Mordecai's word to Esther is an echo of Christ's own words. "For whoever wants to save their life will lose it, but whoever loses their life for me will find it" (Matt. 16:25). This is a Kingdom principle. Esther risked her life for the assurance of God's favor, and her story inspires us to watch for where God is at work so we can join Him.

Are you prepared to go where you're called?

To whom do you turn for wisdom when you have tough choices to make?

What would you give up in order to follow Jesus?

What would you have a hard time letting go of?

Encounter

Have you experienced a specific call from God on your life? Maybe you heard it early on in your life but never got around to answering it. Maybe you've answered it and are living it out now. Or maybe you are still wrestling with how to respond to God's call.

For you, what does it mean to "go with God"? What do you see as the next step in your faith journey? Spend time journaling this question.

The lyrics of the contemporary song "Hear Us from Heaven" (Jared Anderson) read like a psalm. The words recall the cry of holy people who throughout the ages have called to God on behalf of the world. Find this song online and meditate on the lyrics or, better yet, listen. What does this song inspire in you?

WEEK 2: EXERCISE #2

When a computer is told to save a file, it stores the pages randomly wherever there's space. Every time it is asked to go get that file, it finds all the pages and delivers them to you as one complete file. Over time, through thousands of saved files and deletions, those files become more and more fragmented and the computer becomes slower and slower.

That's why we "defrag" our computers every once in a while. Defragmenting gives the operating system the opportunity to regroup, to put things in order again. And what our computers need, our busy lives need. With countless things vying for our attention daily, our chaotic lives need regular defragging to be effective.

Read Ephesians 4:1–6; Psalm 16:5–11; Philippians 3:10–14.

These Scriptures remind us of the importance of keeping the main thing the main thing. Now that you've read these three passages, read them again, this time underlining words and phrases that focus you on what is most important.

Paul tells the Philippians, "I want to know Christ." Have you ever heard yourself say that? Is knowing Christ a priority in your life? How do you express that desire?

In order for you to focus on knowing Christ, what do you need to set aside?

One way Paul has learned to live that passion is by "forgetting what is behind and straining toward what is ahead." One way to "defrag" is making peace with past mistakes and memories, so we can confidently go with God. Have you moved past your past yet?

Now reread these three passages one more time, then with these ideas in mind, write out a prayer in your journal that reflects your desire to focus more on Christ.

Encounter

This is an exercise in honesty. Get out your bank statement or checkbook and your calendar. Look back over the last thirty days and ask yourself what these two pieces of your life say about you. What does your spending say about your priorities? What does your calendar say about your priorities? Journal what you see.

In your journal, make two headings at the top of a page: "temporary" and "eternal." Now, under each heading list of all the things on which you've spent money or time that fit into either category. Power bills are necessary but temporary. Giving to a charitable organization or church has an eternal impact. Playing computer games is temporary. Building a healthy relationship with someone has more lasting consequences.

Where in your life could you use a little "defragging," or regrouping? Where are you encountering Jesus? Journal your experiences.

WEEK 2: EXERCISE #3

Philip was a believer who left Jerusalem to go preach the gospel to the Samaritans. He was successful in Samaria, but God called him away from something that was going well so He could send him down a deserted road to save the soul of one man. Philip found himself on the side of a road just as this Ethiopian man passed by in his chariot.

Read Acts 8:26–40.

The man was a high-ranking official in the Ethiopian government, in charge of the entire treasury. And he was a eunuch (one who has been altered physically in order to give himself completely to whatever work he'd been set apart for). People did not choose to become eunuchs. It was chosen for them. To add insult to injury, eunuchs were not allowed into the Jewish world.

Even though he'd never be allowed into the temple as a eunuch, this man in our story was interested in the Jewish faith. He'd been to Jerusalem and was on his way home when Philip found him. Philip heard him reading the Scripture and asked him if he knew what he was reading. The man looked at the scroll in his lap, then looked at Philip. "How can I understand this, unless someone teaches me?"

Make a list of all the circumstances that seem to have lined up in order for God to reach the heart of this Ethiopian man.

Can you think of a story like this one, of someone who seems to have been led directly into the path of God?

Looking back on your own life, do you see ways that God moved and directed people and circumstances in order to draw you in?

What do you learn about God from this story?

Read Romans 10:14–15.

In your journal, write the following four statements:

1. Preach the gospel where you are.
2. The gospel is both word and deed.
3. Every person deserves a fair account of the gospel. Every person.
4. Search yourself. Make sure nothing stands in the way of someone's salvation.

Now, take a few minutes to meditate on each statement, asking the Spirit of God to speak into your life.

Encounter

Do you have a soft spot for an area of the world, or a people group that's on your heart? Two online resources, Operation World (www.operationworld.org) and Joshua Project (www.joshuaproject.net), can teach you more about areas of the world God might be calling you to learn more about.

Choose one of these sites and go online to look up more about an area of the world or a people group you have an interest in. Learn something about them, then take time today to pray for those who do not yet know Jesus.

WEEK 2: EXERCISE #4

The disciples were intensely curious about the end of time. "Tell us when will this happen and what will be the sign of your coming and of the end of the age?" (Matt. 24:3). They were always asking for details. When? Where? How? Jesus was constantly redirecting their curiosity to better questions.

Read Matthew 24:36–42.

Verse 36 states a very clear promise: no one knows the day or time except the Father. Spending inordinate time and energy calculating the time of the end is a futile pursuit. Matthew 6:25–27 reminds us to not even worry about our life.

What things are you concerned about that are not in your control?

What exactly has worry accomplished in your life?

Where has doubt kept you from taking steps of faith?

Read Matthew 24:43–44; 2 Timothy 4:2.

Jesus will come at an unexpected time. That is a given. What does it mean to be prepared for His coming?

What does it mean to "be ready in season and out of season"?

Read Matthew 24:45–51.

It was a common practice in Jesus' day for the master of a house to leave his servant in charge of the home and other servants. In spiritual terms, who is this passage talking about?

Who is being left in charge of the "house"?

Who is asked to be faithful and wise?

In what ways are we able to influence the future?

Encounter

Do you have a five-year plan for your personal life? Professionals often make short- and long-term goals to guide them toward a more successful career. But it doesn't often occur to us to take the same care with our spiritual lives. Do you have a plan for growth in your spiritual life? Where would you like to be—spiritually speaking—six months from now? A year from now? Five years from now? What, if anything, is standing in the way of your reaching that goal? What steps do you need to take in order to get where you want to go?

Journal on these questions, then take time to talk with Jesus about your spiritual goals.

WEEK 2: EXERCISE #5

In the video teaching, we were given these points for reflection:

1. Jesus wants us to learn how to love the Father.
2. Jesus wants us to hold on to faith, so that no one can take our crown.
3. Jesus wants us to spend our time looking for Him *now*, not in the clouds but in every face, in every person, in every circumstance. Do you have a devotional practice of spending time simply loving the Father?

Read Psalms 96, 98, and 146.

The Psalms teach us how to pray. They show us what an honest hunger for God looks like. They teach us how to respond to spiritual warfare, and they show us how to worship God. Many of the Psalms are outpourings of praise and thanksgiving to God, revealing a deep love for the Father.

If it's true that prayers probably say more about our relationship to God than anything else, then what do your prayers say about your relationship to God?

Encounter

Review the week's exercises. What common themes are emerging? Where did you encounter Jesus this week in the Scriptures? In your devotional moments? Where is God calling you to be faithful? Where is God asking you to take authority? Where is Jesus at work and waiting for you to join Him? Journal these questions.

WEEK 3: EXERCISE #1

Can we *really* live for Jesus? Is it actually possible to get beyond our SELF so we can live for Christ? The apostle Paul thought so. Turn in your Bible to Colossians 3:1–2. Read these two verses. Paul teaches in these lines that as we surrender our lives to Jesus, our thoughts and behaviors will reflect that decision. We are to set our hearts, minds, thoughts, and eyes on Jesus. Anything that prevents us from doing so is sin. Sin is anything that separates us from the Lord. The old and dark keep us from the new and light of Christ, and sometimes it is the subtle stuff that does the most damage to our spiritual growth.

Read Colossians 3:1–2.

Read these two verses aloud.

How does Paul's teaching work in real life? In your journal make two columns. Make the heading of one column "Old/ Dark." This column is for those things in our life that keep us from living the way Jesus wants us to live. These are thoughts and habits that have become a barrier to spiritual growth. In this list, include any behavior or thought pattern more focused on SELF than on God or others. Also list mindsets and even hurts that have kept you from encountering Jesus. Be honest. List things you would not normally want to share in church. This is between you and Jesus.

Now move to the second column. Label it with the heading "New/ Light." Paul tells us that because we have been raised with Christ we are to set our hearts on things above where Christ is seated at the right hand of God. What are the things you hope for, dream of, look for, see, treasure, desire, give, and love? This list is for the habits in your life that point to Christ. These don't necessarily represent accomplishments so much as efforts or desires to move in the right direction.

Take time right now to complete these two lists. Ask God to reveal to you the places in your life you might not usually acknowledge as barriers or blessings.

Encounter

Now that you have your list, place it in the presence of God. See yourself sitting before God—the One Who Loves You Most. Hold each item up before Him and ask Him to reveal to you the source of these wounds, habits, or memories. Ask for forgiveness if you need to. Ask Him to give you strength to make changes in your life where they are needed. Ask God for courage and strength to move forward—into the light. Ask Him to forgive you for pitching tents in the dark.

For each item that represents a move in the right direction, give thanks to God for progress. Celebrate with Him those practices, people, and purposes that encourage you to live in the Kingdom of Christ. And acknowledge that even in light of your best and worst, God loves you so dearly. In Christ, there is no shame!

Before leaving this place of prayer, allow God to respond to your prayers by reading aloud the promise of 2 Corinthians 12:9. "But he said to me, 'My grace is sufficient for you, for my power is made perfect in weakness.'

Therefore I will boast all the more gladly about my weaknesses, so that Christ's power may rest on me." How does this verse inform your life?

Memorize 2 Corinthians 12:9. You might even want to write it in big letters across the lists you've made, as a promise that seals both the good and bad with God's creative grace.

WEEK 3: EXERCISE #2

Amazing Grace! How sweet the sound, that saved a wretch like me! I once was lost, but now am found, was blind, but now I see.

—*John Newton (1725–1807)*

"John Newton, Clerk; once an infidel and libertine, a servant of slaves in Africa, was by the rich mercy of our Lord and Saviour Jesus Christ preserved, restored, pardoned, and appointed to preach the faith he had long labored to destroy."

These words are inscribed on John Newton's tombstone. Newton was the son of a sea captain who joined his father's ship at the age of eleven. His mother died when he was very young. He led an immoral life, full of rebellion and failure. "He was rejected by his father, in trouble with all his employers, and finally jailed and degraded. In later years he served on slave ships, where he so incurred the hatred of his employer's Negro wife that he became virtually a slave of slaves."[1]

His actual conversion was the result of a violent storm in which he almost lost his life. Surviving the storm, John Newton became a minister at the age of thirty-nine. He gave the rest of his life to serving God. During that time he wrote many hymns and never forgot the experience of being shaken to the core when he almost died. He relished the undeserving grace and forgiveness he received for all his sins. John's heart was profoundly stirred by the fact that Jesus died for him because He *loved* him. In the light of that saving grace, Newton stood amazed.

Read Ephesians 2:8–9. Now read it again, this time substituting your own name for the personal pronouns in the passage (i.e., "It is by grace, *Carolyn* has been saved"). Does personalizing the truth of this passage deepen its meaning for you? How does this message amaze you?

Encounter

Describe an experience in your life that shook you to the core. Journal the memory of that experience. Where were you in that time of your life? Where was God? What questions were you left with? As you look again at that experience, do you see ways God might have worked positively through that season to build character or faith into your life? Not that God *caused* it, but that He worked *through* it? Where do you sense assurance of God's presence?

WEEK 3: EXERCISE #3

Read Genesis 1:3–4; Job 12:22; 1 John 1:5–7; 2 Corinthians 4:6; Revelation 22:5.

Compare the themes of these passages. How are light and darkness described or contrasted?

Who are the main players in all these Scriptures?

What do you learn about light as you read these passages?

List the places the light shines.

Read John 3:19–21.

This passage is in the same paragraph as what is arguably the most recognizable verse in the Bible: John 3:16. And as powerful as John 3:16 is, these verses that follow are every bit as profound and practical. John teaches us here the fundamental truth of light and dark. In the spirit realm, things left in the dark are under the control of the enemy, who loves the cover of darkness. In the dark, he can deceive and lie. Things brought into the light are under the control of Jesus and in the realm of truth. No wonder we're encouraged in the Scripture to confess! Confession isn't about shame or guilt! It is about bringing our weaknesses under the power of Jesus, who loves us and is on our side.

Are there memories or habits in your life still lurking in the darkness?

Can you see how the secrets in your life are controlled by the enemy?

What steps do you need to take in order to bring every part of your life into the light of Christ?

Encounter

Music can stir the soul in a very tender way. Some songs make such an impression on us that just the tune hummed years later will evoke all kinds of emotion. A love song from our teen years can bring back strong memories beyond the song itself. A hymn may evoke feelings of security if your church memories are warm (likewise, if your growing-up church experience was not so great, a hymn can evoke a visceral reaction).

Is there a song from your early life (sacred or secular) that has strong emotions attached to it—either good or bad? What comes to mind when you remember this song? Is there a song that encourages your spirit? Write the lyrics of that song in your journal and reflect on why it means something to you. If you can, sing it as an offering to God. Thank God for music and art that bring light into life and give expression to our deepest feelings.

WEEK 3: EXERCISE #4

Our teaching comes from John's Gospel where he tells of a miracle healing by Jesus of a man born blind. Read the whole story in John 9 now. After you read the story, we'll continue with a closer look at the various scenes.

Read John 9:1–12.

In the culture of Jesus' day, to be blind likely meant being resigned to a life of begging; otherwise, you'd starve. When they meet this blind man, the disciples see the same man on the road that Jesus sees. He is sitting by the road begging, pleading, maybe even desperate. Listening for sympathetic voices, craning for someone nearby who might give him something. This is a man in need. Yet, because of their cultural biases, the disciples who see him have questions but no help. When they look at him, they only see "sin."

Jesus, on the other hand, sees an opportunity for transformation. He talks with him, touches him, then commands him to "go and wash." The man is so transformed by the experience that people who have known him his whole life no longer recognize him. This is the effect of going from darkness to light! The miracle happens in a moment; the effect of this encounter with Jesus will last a lifetime.

Describe the extent of this man's healing. What changes for him the day he encounters Jesus? Think about his lifestyle, his mental state, his relationships, his spiritual life. Think what it meant for this man to go from a dependent life to freedom. Journal the change.

How are the disciples changed by this experience? What perspective shifts do they encounter as Jesus engages this man and heals him? How does that mature their understanding of Jesus?

Read John 9:13–34.

In verse 13 we read that the man born blind is still being led by others. We also notice that his life is beginning to change. Light is taking over darkness. Note that his transformation is a process, not an event (sound familiar?).

In verse 14, we find treasure! Here is the reason for bringing the man before the Pharisees. And here is why Jesus uses His own spit. Remember that this miracle takes place on the Jewish Sabbath. One of the oral traditions of the Pharisees—a tradition they elevated to the same level of authority as the Holy Scriptures—was that "they forbade anyone to spit on the Sabbath lest the spit run downhill and make mud."[2]

And yet, Jesus uses His own spit to heal a man, then He sends him to the Pool of Siloam. This pool is situated right in the middle of the crowds gathered for the Feast. That's no coincidence! This is not Jesus' usual, quiet miracle-making. This is Jesus making a point. And making it loud and clear.

The real treasure is not in the healing. It is in the mud and in the Sabbath! "Remember the Sabbath and keep it holy." That was the irreducible law of the Pharisees. In their quest to keep the laws, they had become blind to the real needs of real people. They'd lost the heart of God in the letter of the law.

Every age faces this danger. In our culture, in our time, what are the risks that might leave us spiritually blind?

What one thing do you know now (that you may not have always known) that has helped you to see?

How might you make the main lesson of this section—that legalism can keep us blind to the needs of others—into a personal prayer? Write that prayer in your journal.

Read John 9:35–41.

Jesus seeks out the man and is now asking the questions. The miracle happened in a moment in the beginning of the chapter but the transformation of his heart was a gradual change as the man born blind began to really see Jesus for who He was.

In verse 37, Jesus says this in response to the man's question about the Son of Man: "You have now seen him; in fact, he is the one speaking with you." The Greek word used here for "seen" is *horao* and denotes the "physical act of seeing and gives prominence to the discerning mind."[3]

Horao is the perfect word for what has just happened. The man now sees in the physical sense of that term, but he also discerns truth as he hasn't before. His blindness was not just physical, for now he proclaims Jesus as Lord and worships Him. His inner eyes have been opened to a revelation of *the* Jesus!

Read John 3:19–21.

John teaches us that light and dark cannot occupy the same space. Those things we leave in the dark (hoping we can hold on to our old habits and old self) will be under the control of our spiritual enemy. Those things we bring into the light will be exposed to Jesus for healing and transformation.

Given the offer on the table, what keeps people in the dark?

What is keeping *you* in the dark?

Encounter

Life moves fast. We fill our twenty-four hours and wish we had more. Taking time to enjoy the moment is a rare skill. We are much more likely to go from moment to multitasking. One of the lessons of this story is in the disciples' response to the man born blind. They asked the wrong question about his life. We, too, are prone to ask the wrong questions because we don't slow down enough to see what we're actually looking at. One of the hallmarks of the emotionally mature spiritual life is the ability to slow down so we can be more effective in the things we do.

Today, would you be willing to take ten minutes to enjoy either the sunset or the sunrise? Turn off your phone, set your iPad aside, and simply sit and watch. Then journal your experience. What do you notice about the light and the darkness?

WEEK 3: EXERCISE #5

Okay, so we've been shaken *and* stirred . . . now what? In our story of Jesus and the blind man, there is a directive. Imbedded in the blind man's healing is the instruction to "go." That's a command for all of us. In Matthew 28:19, Jesus tells His followers to "go and make disciples of all nations." The spiritual equation is this: change = charge. When an encounter with Jesus changes us, we are charged to go and share what we've received. Jesus is ours but not ours to hoard.

Change = charge. As the Word shapes you, how can you live out this spiritual equation in the coming week? Whom can you serve? What can you do together with your group to reach beyond yourselves? One group helped a family move in to their new home (not a family that attends their church!). Another person bought Bibles at a yard sale and gave them away. Two women made casseroles and delivered them to an elderly woman in need.

How will you respond to Jesus' command to "go"? Choose a project that puts you face to face with someone in need. Make it doable (grand plans are wonderful, but seldom make it off the drawing board). Learn the names of those you serve. Stay in touch. Build a relationship.

Encounter

What key principle have you learned from this story? Write a personal prayer that reflects this principle and your desire to see it lived out in your life.

Note the steps in healing of the man born blind. First, Jesus went to him. Then He struck up a conversation. From there, physical healing happened. Gradually, the man's heart was changed. The next time Jesus encountered him, the man was able to see Jesus for who He was. Then he worshipped.

What things in your life do you have the power to change? Which of these do you need to seriously consider overcoming for the sake of physical or spiritual health? Eating? Smoking? Language? Jealousy? Anger? What help do you need in order to overcome those habits?

What things in your life do you have no control over? Pray for God to give you peace in the midst of those situations.

Find the Serenity Prayer online (google "serenity prayer") and read it as a prayer today. Print it out and stick it on your fridge or bathroom mirror.

WEEK 4: EXERCISE #1

Read 2 Corinthians 1.

Yes! When it comes to the promises of God, this is our final, glorious answer. In 2 Corinthians 1:20, Paul tells us that no matter how many promises God has made they are all *yes!* in Christ Jesus. In this lesson, we will be led into an awareness of the mercy and grace Jesus reflected in the promises of God.

Read Ruth 1–4 and Matthew 1:1–17.

Ruth is a beautiful story of God's provision. The genealogy found in Matthew 1 is so often overlooked as a boring list, when in fact it is a beautiful map of God's promises fulfilled.

How do you encounter Jesus in these Scriptures? How do these two journeys (Ruth's journey, and the journey from Abraham to Jesus) give you hope for today?

What promises do you encounter in these two passages of Scripture? Make a list in your journal.

Encounter

Revisit the list of promises made from the above exercise. Where has God kept that same promise in your life? Jot down some examples of how the Lord has kept His promises to you, then after each promise, write, "YES!"

WEEK 4: EXERCISE #2

Ask most people how their lives are right now, and chances are they'll use terms like "stressed out," "busy," or "overwhelmed." It's no wonder. We are covered over by schoolwork, housework, yardwork, errands, food, meetings, exercise, church, devotional time, football games, hockey games, travel, music, bills, pets, cars, parents, kids. Not to mention whatever it is you do in order to support all those habits and responsibilities. And we are so remarkably accessible: cell phone, home phone, Facebook, texting, e-mail, Twitter.

What a life. No wonder we are all so tired! No wonder our relationships are suffering. We've become slaves to a culture that not only sets the pace but teaches us how to run: go all out until you burn out. Don't stop until you win or until it's done or until you die, whichever comes first.

Wouldn't you like another word for your life than stressed out, overworked, overwhelmed? Gandhi once said, "There is more to life than simply increasing its speed."

Read Isaiah 40.

Isaiah gets us. He writes eloquently about the state of life, the uncertainties we feel, and the power of trust in a great God. This passage teaches us a lot about the character of God. Trusting in the character of who God is and putting our whole confidence in Him even in the midst of adversity is our ticket to peace. We discover in this passage that it isn't about having all the answers, but trusting in the One who does.

God is who He says He is, the Great I AM, The Light of the World. Even in the darkest hours we can trust in Him.

Read through Isaiah 40 again, this time underlining or highlighting all the words and phrases that speak of God's character. What phrases display the authority of God? Where do you encounter Jesus in this Old Testament Scripture?

There is a powerful word here for those of us who are overwhelmed by the pace of this world: Wait on the Lord. God knows how fast we are created to go. He knows that in some seasons, we'll be ready to fly like an eagle. Other times, we'll be grateful for strength to run without growing weary. And at times, it will be enough to walk without fainting. Knowing ourselves—and our God—is the trick to setting a holy pace.

What new insights from this chapter in Isaiah helps you to trust God's care over your life? In what ways have you seen the Lord work in your life in the past month, week, or day that helped you understand who He is? Make a few notes in your journal.

Encounter

If you've got the capability on your cell phone, program an alert with this phrase: "God is like . . ." Schedule it to remind you often during the day to complete the sentence. Notice how your surroundings inform your responses.

If you're not a phone junkie, you can accomplish the same goal with Post-it notes. Write "God is like . . ." on several Post-its and place them on your bathroom mirror, computer, above the kitchen sink, on the radio dial of your car . . . wherever you spend time. Each time a note catches your eye, complete the sentence.

Don't just do this for a day; do it for a week. The goal is to realign your thoughts around the nature and goodness of God. Journal what you've learned. What did you learn about God through this experience that you can share with someone?

WEEK 4: EXERCISE #3

One time Jesus healed a madman who lived among the tombs of Gerasenes, a region of ten cities. Reading this story in Mark, we encounter two important spiritual principles: (1) Jesus heals. (2) True healing brings freedom.

Read Mark 5:1–17.

Jesus came to a city by boat, got out, and was met by a man who'd been hovering nearby among the tombs. This was not just any man. He was the poorest of the poor, living among the dead. He was the kind of guy the community tolerated but avoided. Back when people noticed him, he had often been chained but no chain was strong enough to hold him. Now, he wandered alone among the tombs and hills beyond the city, unchained but in agony.

Night and day he cried out and cut himself. The pain of the cuts on the outside of his body masked the internal pain. Even today, "cutting" is a way that many people deal with deep, emotional wounds and scars no one sees but Jesus. In fact, this is a growing trend among teens but is certainly not limited by age. And it is only one of many ways we use unhealthy habits to cope with our internal wounds. Some of us cope by self-medicating with drugs or alcohol. Still others agonize under the weight of eating disorders or by withdrawing socially.

What is your usual response to pain or suffering? Do you pull in, reach out, or draw back?

Are you dealing right now with an unhealthy response to life's disappointments? Have you taken this to Jesus? Have you shared it with a spiritual partner who can help you pray through to a better place?

Read Mark 5:7–8.

This story of the man Jesus healed is a great example of Jesus' influence over demons. In verses 7–8, we see the fear He invokes as the demon sees Jesus coming. And then we encounter Jesus' authority in the spiritual realm as He speaks deliverance into this man's life. No magic, no fanfare, just two words: "Come OUT." When the One who holds the keys of hell and death speaks, no demon is safe!

Read Mark 5:9–10.

All kinds of voices contend for our attention. Real voices, like those of our kids, spouses, bosses; but also voices of the world—temptations and ambitions. All those voices try to convince us they will bring happiness. On our rough days, they wear us down. Other voices bring feelings of worthlessness, doubt, fear, shame, failure. These are the voices of disgrace.

And in the midst of all those other voices, there is always one other voice—the voice of grace. That is the voice of Jesus, the still, quiet voice that calls us to a higher place.

What does the voice of Jesus sound like in your life? Have you learned to discern it? Have you trained your inner ear to hear that voice when it speaks into your life?

Read Psalm 46:10.

Write it on a Post-it and put it in a place where you will see it when you are likely to be stressed out. "Be still and know that I am God," the psalmist tells us. When the world is yelling, when the voices compete for our attention, be still. When everything in us tells us we have too much to do and not enough time to do it, be still. When the battles rage, our greatest weapon is to be still and call on the name of Jesus.

Read Mark 5:11–13.

Notice that the demons ask Jesus to send them into the pigs that were grazing nearby. In His presence, they were unable to possess a pig without permission. This is an important point. In the presence of Jesus, demons must submit. His authority in the spiritual realm is absolute. This is why we want to bring Jesus into even the darkest places in us. Only Jesus has ultimate power over the powers and principalities of darkness.

Read 1 Corinthians 10:13.

Some of our demons are harder to let go of than others. We will say we are "struggling" with something, but honestly . . . we just don't want to let go of it yet. Maybe we have acknowledged it as an issue, but we are still allowing it to run around in our lives, wreaking havoc. We rationalize. We say it's just too strong a demon to be destroyed. But Paul teaches us that no temptation has overtaken us that isn't common or conquerable. Whatever the issue, God will not give us anything we cannot bear, and when we are tempted He will always provide a way out.

In other words, that thing you're dealing with is not bigger than God! Nor is it somehow separate from your relationship with God. Paul tells us God is the one knocking down walls and making doorways. Our part is to walk through. Because (and this is the real point) *you can't stay where you are and go with God at the same time.*

What deep wound, what root of bitterness, what pain has taken hold in the depth of your soul that Jesus wants to reveal to you and heal and cleanse you from? Will you allow Him full access to your heart and habits so you can be finally and fully free?

Remember: *there is no shame in Christ!*

Read Mark 5:14–17.

Fear is so often the *natural* (not supernatural) response to deliverance. We don't like change so most of the time we fight it, even if we ask for it. In the story of Jesus and the demoniac, fear takes over and the people ask Jesus to leave. With a clear choice between demons and the Savior of the world, they have chosen their demons. All because they were afraid to change.

Sound familiar? Paul tells us (2 Tim. 1:7) that we have not been given a spirit of fear but of power, love, and self-discipline. Power, love, and self-discipline are the weapons with which we fight the enemy who so wants to control our minds.

Make the words of 2 Timothy 1:7 into a prayer that you can memorize and pray daily.

Read Psalm 146.

Only God! This is the great proclamation of the psalmist. God is Creator and Redeemer, our one and only true God. Psalm 146 advises us to trust our God, because *only* He can be trusted. Only He remains faithful forever. Humans, no matter how influential and well-intentioned, will eventually disappoint.

Only God! Psalm 146 paints an amazingly accurate picture of the Messiah we know to be Jesus Christ. This Messiah, who has been there since creation, has now come in human form to uphold the cause of the oppressed, set prisoners free, give food to the hungry and sight to the blind. Our Jesus cares about the ones in the margins, defending them against the wicked. Jesus will turn the world upside down to redeem one of His own!

And *you* are one of His own. Jesus wants to redeem your past. Jesus has come to restore the years the locusts have eaten. Jesus wants to make something beautiful out of your tears. Where we see only dead ends, He sees possibilities.

Encounter

Where are you in this healing journey? Are you just beginning? Halfway there? Almost home? Are your problems legion, or are you beginning to see progress?

(NOTE: This assignment could take a while. It may be something you want to begin today, then continue to work on throughout the rest of this study.)

In your journal, draw a timeline. Begin with your earliest memory and end with today. Now, note those places on your timeline where you've seen progress toward a healed life. A moment when you gave or received forgiveness might be noted, or a moment when you encountered Jesus in a retreat setting or study. Use just a word or two to note a few of your more significant moments of healing.

Now, take a few minutes to offer your timeline to God as a prayer of praise. Thank Him for progress made.

WEEK 4: EXERCISE #4

Read Mark 5:18–20.

The scene of our story shifts as Jesus heads back to the boat. Out of a spirit of fear, the people of the region have asked Jesus to leave them. The man, now healed, begs to go with Him. He has experienced real freedom and now he is spiritually hungry. He wants to follow Jesus into this new life.

The Hebrew word for "mercy" is *hesed*. This is not an easy word to translate. It can mean grace or compassion, or sometimes loving-kindness or thankfulness. The idea is that God's grace toward us—His patience and loyalty—come out of His love for us. The corresponding Greek word is *charis*, which means something like unmerited favor or simply, "thanks." *Hesed* is God's loving response to our imperfect lives. Our Father gave us His best in Jesus, even when we did not deserve it, He gave us His all, His everything, instead of what we deserved. That's mercy. That's grace. That's Jesus!

And that's who this man who was healed was ready to talk about. He was ready to share his story of this Jesus, who gave him another chance at life.

Interestingly, the disciples are silent in this story. As far as we know, they never even left the boat. These are the same men who just saw Jesus calm a storm out on the water. They have just asked, "Who is this that the wind and the waves obey him?" And now on shore, they have witnessed the demons obeying His voice. And they have witnessed the transformation of a man. And yet, they are silent.

If you were a disciple on this journey, what would your reaction be? Heading home at the end of this trip, what would you share with your family, with your friends?

Where are you seeing Jesus at work in your life, or in the world around you? How are you sharing those stories with others? Are you telling the story of Jesus?

Why do you suppose Jesus wanted the man to stay in this town? What blessings would he have missed if Jesus had allowed the man to go with Him? For so long, this man was isolated, living among tombs. Now he is asked to stay among the very people who rejected him. Do you see how this might have been part of his healing?

Encounter

With whom do you most identify in the Scripture of Mark 5:1–20? The madman, the disciples, the townspeople? Do you want to stay in your comfort zone, in the boat, in town, standing on the shore, or sitting at the feet of Jesus?

If we're honest about it, most of us are a mixed bag. We can relate to the guy who got healed, but we can also relate to the crowd that got scared and the disciples who stayed quiet. Journal on this thought. What are the healing stories in your life waiting to be told? What parts of your life are still ruled by fear? Where are you too comfortable to move forward with Jesus?

Read Romans 8:28–39. What is the promise of this passage? How do you relate this promise to the principles of the story in Mark 5? How will you claim this promise of protection and presence over your life?

WEEK 4: EXERCISE #5

Turn to John 8:31–36. Read these passages slowly and commit them to memory.

How do these verses connect with the passage in Mark? Write down your thoughts.

Jesus tells His audience in John 8 that true freedom is not just the sum total of our circumstances. True freedom is a spiritual reality that transforms our lives, no matter what our details are. It is truth, He says, that sets us free. And truth is not a set of laws. Truth is a person. Truth is in Christ, who has come to set us free not just from uncomfortable circumstances but at a much more fundamental level. Jesus Christ sets us free from slavery to sin. He sets us free from slavery to shame and guilt. He sets us free from slavery to fear and death.

Read Galatians 5:13–15.

Spiritual freedom is not the absence of boundaries. It is the pursuit of holiness, grounded in love. Translated into a prayer, Galatians 5:13 might read, "Give us the power of Kingdom restraint." Or as Jesus taught us to pray (Matt. 6:13), "Lead us not into temptation, but deliver us from the evil one." This is a prayer for holiness to invade us. In other words, "Take my thoughts captive, God, so I'm not constantly having to battle every choice. Give me some holy boundaries I can operate out of so I'm not always having to choose between what I want and what I can give, and so I'm not always having to wrestle between my shallowness and Your depth."

Be honest with yourself. When you pray, "And lead us not into temptation," do you actually mean for God to destroy every obstacle and deliver you from every demon that stands between you and holiness? Or in reality, are you praying something more like: "And lead me not into temptation . . . because I can find it all by myself"?

Are you living like a free person, or are you bound spiritually to forces that work against your relationship to Jesus?

Encounter

Jesus came to set us free. Do you believe it, even if you cannot see it?

Write this verse at the top of your journal page: "If the Son sets you free, you will be free indeed" (John 8:36).

What do you think this verse meant to its original audience? When Jesus talked about freedom, what do you think the people heard?

What does this verse mean to you? In what areas of your life have you been set free? In what areas do you need to pray for freedom?

What one practical step will you take in response to this study? Is God calling you to have a different relationship to your stuff, or to other people, or to your thoughts and habits? Is God calling you to not just sit there but do something, to participate in the in-breaking Kingdom?

WEEK 5: EXERCISE #1

My heart has heard you say, "Come and talk with me."
And my heart responds, "LORD, I am coming."

—*Psalm 27:8 (NLT)*

Hearing God's voice is a spiritual practice that requires exercise. We learn to hear as we listen to Scripture, the experiences of others (present and past), and our own prayers. Unless we intentionally train our inner or "spiritual" ear to hear, we will too easily let the voice of God pass by totally unnoticed. Or we may think we've heard Him but we receive the message tentatively because we feel ourselves somehow unworthy.

The practice of listening prayerfully to the Spirit's leading is rooted in silence and sacrifice. It is cultivated over time as we allow the Lord to use us in His Kingdom work. Listening happens as we make ourselves quiet and available.

Read 1 Samuel 3:1–18.

Find a quiet place for reading this passage. Be still. Pray, "Lord, give me ears to hear You and a heart to receive all You have for me today." Now, read the Scripture slowly, underlining phrases that repeat or are significant to you.

What are your initial insights? What do you notice about Samuel's encounter with God? What do you notice about how God gets Samuel's attention (note the changes in verses 7 and 21)?

Do you have a personal story of a time when you sensed God's presence and power—even before you were aware of Him in your life?

"He is the LORD; let him do what is good in his eyes" (1 Sam. 3:18). Do you trust God's plan to reveal Himself to His people in His time? Do you trust Him to reveal Himself to your people (your spouse, your children, your coworkers) in His time?

Encounter

Maggie Gobran, a nominee for the 2012 Nobel Peace Prize, works with the poorest of the poor in Cairo, Egypt. "Mama Maggie," as she's known among the poor, reaches out to children living in garbage dumps, offering the love and hope that come only through Christ. She is a woman of deep prayer who has learned the great value of silence in the quest for the heart of God. Mama Maggie has written, "Silence your body to listen to your words, silence your tongue to listen to your thoughts, silence your thoughts to listen to your heart beating, silence your heart to listen to your spirit, and silence your spirit you listen to His spirit. In silence you leave many and be with The One."[4]

Let's try a timed listening exercise that brings us to a place of silence and into the company of The One.

In this encounter, you will spend five minutes in silence. Don't try too hard to make something spiritual happen in these minutes. Just listen. Be aware of anything you hear—traffic noise, sounds of children, the on-and-off click of air-conditioning, your heartbeat. Listen to your own thoughts and be aware of the directions they take.

At the end of these moments of listening, record in your journal what you've heard.

Now think about the noise of a usual day. What fills the air around you? Family talks, television, YouTube, music, phone calls? Think through a day and write down as many typical sounds as come to mind.

How might God be speaking to you through these people or things? How are these noises distracting you from the voice of God?

Where in your day could you develop the discipline of silence so you're more able to hear the voice of God? Would you be willing to commit to a ten- or fifteen-day experiment, in which you give at least ten minutes per day to the discipline of listening?

Write a statement of understanding around the notion of silence or listening as a "fertilizer" for spiritual soil.

WEEK 5: EXERCISE #2

Read Philippians 4:14–20.

Paul is writing to the people in Philippi, for whom he has a special affection. Paul was the founder of the Philippian church and spent a considerable amount of time there. When he wrote to them, he wanted to acknowledge their generosity while he was in prison and encourage them in the faith.

Reread this passage and circle or underline all the words and phrases related to giving (i.e., share, giving, receiving, fragrant offering, etc.). Now, make a list in your journal of the words and terms you've circled. Take a few minutes to look these words up in a dictionary. How do these definitions inform your understanding of giving? Out of what spirit do the Philippians give? In what spirit is it received? What do you learn here about joy?

Generosity and passion are marks of one who has had a genuine encounter with Christ. We are called to give generously of ourselves—time, talent, gifts, prayers, and witness. We are called, out of our deep love for Jesus, to go and spread the seeds of this good news of redemption. And we are challenged to trust God with our needs. Our giving in every way is a fragrant offering to Him.

Encounter

Review the parable of the four soils in Luke 8:4–21.

In your journal, make a grid of four boxes. Label the first box on the top left-hand corner "hard soil." Label the box next to it on the top right "rocky soil." Label the bottom left-hand corner box "thorny soil," and label the bottom right-hand box "good soil."

Now, consider all the things that make up your life—family, job, friendships, associations, hobbies, habits. Think, too, about how you spend your time, talents, money, and personal influence. Using the four boxes you've just made, how would you categorize each of these things in your life? Build a list in each box.

As we said earlier, we are all a mixed bag of "sanctified" and "getting there." Some areas of our life bear more spiritual fruit than others. Think of these four boxes you've just made as a map of your spiritual life. Turn them into a prayer journey, taking time with each list for praise, intercession, and confession.

Remember: Life is a journey. None of us has yet arrived. All of us are sowing the seeds, plowing in the seeds, pulling the weeds, and mining the rocks. Staying true to the process is the key to growing roots and bearing fruit.

Read Philippians 1:3–6 as you close your prayer time. Give thanks to God for those who have made an impact on your life and have helped you to grow.

WEEK 5: EXERCISE #3

Read Romans 12:1.

Let's shift for a moment to this brief verse in Romans. Paul urges his audience here to give everything, even their bodies, to God in response to His mercy. In this verse, we can hear echoes of many healing stories—the stories of Joanna and Mary Magdelene among them, who gave themselves to the work and wonder of following Jesus in response to the healing and mercy they received from Him.

"Make yourselves a living sacrifice." This is what it means to abandon our lives to Christ. It means following Jesus. It means giving up our own place for the sake of His journey. On this road, we find our value in the ways we sacrifice our time, effort, and comforts for the sake of building something eternal. Such sacrifice changes the very texture of the soil of our hearts.

2 Corinthians 12:15 says, "I will very gladly spend for you everything I have and expend myself as well." This is the attitude of one who follows Jesus.

The hard part of sacrifice is that it changes us, and no one really likes change. But the wonderful part of sacrifice is that . . . it changes us! We begin to take on more and more of the character of Christ. We take on His interests as we shed our own. We learn to love like He loves. We begin to see the world around us as Jesus sees it. It is a glorious transformation.

Reflect on the phrase "living sacrifice." For a community of faith used to making animal sacrifices, how would this term have been received? What do you think it might have meant, in a first-century context?

Do you know someone who you'd say has given themselves as a "living sacrifice"?

Read 2 Corinthians 12:15; 1 Samuel 7:1–12.

Highlight or underline all the words in these two passages that describe the attitude of a follower of Jesus. What does this list teach you about yourself and your own walk with Jesus?

What changes do you need to commit to, so you can move forward?

Maybe this is the key question for all of us who truly want transformation: Why is change so *hard*?

Janet Hagberg has written on the stages of faith.[5] With each stage, we grow in our understanding of God and ourselves, but along the way we will face the temptation to stop moving forward. Why? Because no one really likes change. Yet, it is as we press in to Jesus, as we allow transformation to happen, that we discover our heart's deepest desires.

Encountering Jesus is really about discovering who we are.

Read 1 Samuel 7:1–12.

An Old Testament practice teaches us how to stop and acknowledge those times when we have encountered God, experienced His provision, and moved forward. Often, when the people of God were journeying toward their destiny, they would encounter the Lord and mark the occasion and place with a rock or pile of rocks.

When Samuel and his people faced a great army of Philistines, Samuel took a stone and set it up in the place of that battle and he named it Ebenezer, for he said, "Thus far, the LORD has helped us" (v. 12).

Encounter

Here, I raise mine Ebenezer, hither by thy help I'm come.

And I hope by thy good pleasure safely to arrive at home.

—from the hymn, "Come, Thou Fount of Every Blessing"

written by Robert Robinson, 1735–1790

There are times when it is right to stop and remember God's real, holy presence. We are here because of God . . . because of His love, His power, His provision, His grace, His goodness.

Begin by going outside to collect a few rocks. Next, make a list in your journal of your own "Ebenezers." What spiritual markers can you note— events, healing moments, or times of provision to which you can point, saying, "Thus far, the Lord has been good to me"? How did your spiritual life mature through these events?

Now, with your rocks in your hand, begin reflecting with God on your spiritual journey. For each significant event noted, drop one of your rocks into a bowl or make a pile in the center of your desk or table. Each time you place a rock in the pile say, "Thus far, the Lord has been good to me."

End this time of thanksgiving and praise by singing all the verses of "Come, Thou Fount of Every Blessing." You can find it online by typing the title into a search engine.

WEEK 5: EXERCISE #4

Read Luke 8:1–4.

Let's look at the parable of the sower in context. Luke introduces us to Jesus' parable in chapter 8 by sharing His location and who He is traveling with. Who is Jesus traveling with? Underline all the different people mentioned in these verses.

Why do you suppose Luke gets specific about the identity of these women?

What do the Scriptures reveal about these three women? Make a list of what you observe.

At least some of these were the same women who encountered the risen Christ and then delivered that resurrection message to the male disciples. They gave their lives to serving the good news and following Jesus.

Can you imagine what it was like to be among the last to see Jesus on the cross, among the first to see the resurrected Christ, and among the ones charged to "go and tell the others"? The women who were with Jesus had that honor.

Knowing something about their circumstances, how do these women encourage you?

Read Luke 8:4–8.

As crowds begin to gather and grow, Jesus encounters all kinds of people on all kinds of journeys. He knows what is in their hearts, so He begins to teach them how to examine their own lives. Jesus gets it that some get it and some don't. Some would rather be part of the crowd. Some are hungry for an experience from God.

Jesus begins talking about a farmer who sows some seed. For an audience familiar with farming, this is a funny story. The farmer is tossing seed everywhere! Evidently cost is not an issue. Nor is fruit. The farmer just tosses, with no concern for where the seed might fall.

Normally, a sower in biblical times would have plowed as he sowed, mixing the seed into the ground. Not so this farmer. He simply sowed. And in those days, two kinds of seeds were generally used: wheat and barley. The barley was sown into poorer soil, and the wheat was for more fertile soil. But our farmer in the parable seems to be sowing the same seed on all soil.[6]

List the ways you witness God's grace in this story.

This story says as much about God's grace as it does about us. Our God is eternally hopeful on our behalf, sowing preveniently into our lives even before we are spiritually ready. He sows into imperfect soil. And our God is eternally generous, giving His best to all His children without preference. The poor—and the poor in spirit—all receive the same seed. One Lord, one faith, one baptism (Eph. 4:5).

Our part in this process is to examine our "soil." Into what is the Spirit of God being sowed? Are there rocks needing to be removed? Weeds that need to be pulled? What needs to be plowed under, what hard soil needs to be broken up? How do we participate in preparing the soil?

An interesting side note: The Pharisees do not seem to be present for this teaching. The hardest soil is not around! The religious guys have been so present and pesky, always hovering nearby watching for Jesus to slip up. Because they are not here for this teaching, Jesus is able to focus on those who have ears to hear.

How does this encourage the disciples?

What encouragement does this give you?

Read Luke 8:9–15.

In verse 9 Jesus' disciples ask Him what this parable means. Jesus is clear in His explanation: He is talking about us. These are the realities present in any journey of faith. The seed is the Word of God sown expectantly into every kind of life. Weeds, rocks, and hard soil are the worries of the world and tools of the enemy, all conspiring against us and keeping the Word of God from taking root.

Following Jesus is about cultivating our spiritual soil, uprooting the weeds of worry, and plowing through the barriers to growth. It is about fertilizing our lives with God's plan, provision, protection, and promises so our roots grow deep into Him who is our Head.

Cultivating soil is about choosing to believe and be saved, not on our own strength but on the grace and generosity of the Sower.

What did the disciples have to let go of before they could allow the seed to take root?

What do you need to let go of in order to hold on to what God has for you?

Encounter

In his letter to the Corinthian church, Paul wrote, "I planted the seed, Apollos watered it, but God has been making it grow" (1 Cor. 3:6). God uses people in the process of sowing the good news about Jesus into the world.

Make a list of people (even if just one name) you believe God is waiting to encounter. Don't assume you know their spiritual needs or the condition of their "soil." Instead, sit in God's presence and with one person at a time in mind, ask Him to show you what their deepest needs are and how you can best serve the process of helping them encounter Jesus. Remember: our job is not to cause growth. Our job is to plant and water!

Journal your insights and what you hear.

WEEK 5: EXERCISE #5

Read Luke 9:1–6.

Here in these verses Jesus gives His disciples marching orders. He sends them out to sow some seeds—to proclaim the coming Kingdom as they healed the sick, cast out demons, and cured diseases. The power they took with them was the power of Jesus. Their resources are what has been sown into them—the words of God that had been planted, watered, and were taking root in their hearts. "Take nothing else," Jesus said, "except what you've been given by Me."

Why do you suppose Jesus asked them not to take a bag, money, or even an extra shirt with them? How might it have changed their message if they'd taken things with them? How would it have affected their sense of dependence on God? How would it have affected the perceptions of those they went to serve?

Here's a question: How could the presence of money change the spiritual climate of a mission journey? When well-meaning efforts focus on material needs, do they help or hurt the spiritual conversation? Is Jesus more concerned about the internals or the externals?

Read Luke 11:1–10.

When Jesus sent His disciples out, He charged them with proclaiming the Kingdom of God. Two chapters later, He is teaching them how to pray for the Kingdom of God to invade the earth.

John Smith, an Australian evangelist, in a sermon in 1997, said that when Christ prayed, "Thy kingdom come, thy will be done on earth as it is in heaven," He was offering us a model for intercession on the big scale. He was showing us that whatever is happening in heaven, that's what we ought to be praying for on earth. Are there wars in heaven? No! Then we ought to be praying for an end to all war on earth. Is there racism in heaven? No! Then we ought to be praying against racism here on earth. Is there anger, or hatred, or unbelief? No! Then we ought to be praying against those things here. When we pray heaven onto earth, we know we're praying the will of God.

Jesus teaches us to pray for God's Kingdom to expand. That's a dangerous prayer. If you mean it when you pray it, then God's going to use you to expand His territory. In other words if you're willing, God can employ you in His Kingdom right now.

Do you have neighbors who don't yet know Christ? Or family members? Or friends or coworkers? If you do, that's territory God wants. Are you using your prayers strategically in order to claim that territory for God's Kingdom? "God, may Your Kingdom come soon to my neighbor." "May your Kingdom come soon to my child, my parent, my brother or sister." "May your Kingdom come soon to my spouse, my ex-spouse, my coworker." Your home and your marriage . . . that's also territory God wants. Are you praying for the Lord to claim that territory for His Kingdom? Are you willing to serve a difficult situation with prayer?

"Lord God, may Your Kingdom come soon into every relationship, every life, every system."

Encounter

Meditate on this quote from an anonymous believer:

Indeed the very heart of this work is nothing else but a naked intent toward God for God's own sake. I call it a naked intent because it is utterly disinterested. In this work the perfect artisan does not seek personal gain or exemption from suffering. One desires only God and God alone. One is so fascinated by the God one loves and so concerned that God's will be done on earth that one neither notices nor cares about one's own ease or anxiety. In reality it amounts to a yearning for God, a longing to see and taste God as much as is possible in this life.

"Your kingdom come, your will be done on earth as it is in heaven."

—Jesus, Matthew 6:10

Write the above verse at the top of a journal page. Now, ask yourself: what kinds of things can I expect to find in heaven? What Kingdom ideals am I most passionate about? Where has the soil of my heart been enlightened to desire more of the Kingdom of God and less of the world?

Journal on these questions.

How can you begin praying more strategically for God's Kingdom to come on earth and into the lives of people you love?

The old adage is: Pray the provision, not the problem. Jesus' teaching on prayer teaches us to focus on the potential present in any situation or life. "Your Kingdom come."

In the last encounter, you were asked to write down the names of a few people God might want to use you in reaching. Pray for them again in this encounter with Jesus, focusing not on their problems but on God's provision.

WEEK 6: EXERCISE #1

Even mature followers of Jesus will sometimes struggle with "letting go and letting God." We are conditioned to default to spirits of fear and doubt rather than rising to the level of faith and trust.

Read Matthew 14:22–33.

As you read this story, make note of all the sights, sounds, tastes, textures, and smells you encounter. Note, too, any emotions described. How would you describe Jesus in this story (calm and detached? Actively engaged? Or . . .)? How would you describe the disciples? Keep in mind that they've just come away from a very intense season. They are grieving the loss of John the Baptist and have accomplished the enormous task of feeding five thousand people. They must be exhausted.

The disciples of Jesus often found themselves in the same boat, both literally and figuratively. As a group, they were often reduced to petty competitions or lapses of faith. This story is no exception. With wind and waves battering their boat, they are anxious. Their anxiety turns to terror when they see Jesus walking toward them on the water. Peter stands out as one who wants to trust what he sees. In fact, he wants to follow Jesus into this miracle of faith.

If you were just meeting Peter for the first time in this story, how would you describe him?

As Jesus walks toward them, He "immediately" calms their fears. Peter challenges the situation, asking Jesus to call him out of the boat. It is tempting to focus on Peter's doubt and the fears that caused him to sink. But before we judge too harshly, we must acknowledge that at least he got out of the boat. Even if for a few wobbly steps, Peter—a mere mortal— actually walked on water! That's faith!

If you'd been there, which disciple would you most likely have been? Are you the anxious type, looking for signs that the looming storm might pass? Are you the guy on deck, looking for what you can do or how you can control the situation? Or are you the bold one, looking beyond the boat for where Jesus might be? Are you one who looks to Jesus with trust, or with questions?

Are you Peter, asking Jesus to call you out of the boat? What do you notice about Jesus' response in this Scripture passage?

Read Psalm 46.

Experience this psalm with all your senses—noting sights, sounds, smells, tastes, textures.

As with our story in Matthew 14, this psalm begins with a storm ("its waters roar and foam") and ends with calm ("Be still, and know that I am God"). What promises do you hear in this psalm?

What instructions do you receive from it for dealing with the storms of life?

Encounter

Be still, and know that I am God.

—Psalm 46:10

Let's make a list. On one side of the page write, "Is this a place where God has me waiting on HIM?" On the other side write "Is this the place where God is waiting on ME?"

Say, for instance, you are discerning your future in your current job. Maybe there are strained office relationships, financial concerns, opportunities to advance, job responsibilities you don't like, or ones you might want to take on. With each element of your situation, ask, "Is this a place where God has me waiting on Him? Or is this a place where God is waiting on me?"

Sit comfortably for a few moments, calming your spirit before the Lord. With your list before you, begin to transform it into a prayer of confession and hope. In what areas of your life do you need to trust the Lord completely with His plan as you wait on Him? In what areas do you need to step out of the boat?

WEEK 6: EXERCISE #2

Read Psalm 116:1–7 and Psalm 118:1–7.

Our most basic need as humans is to know we've been heard. The Psalms teach us that when we talk to Him, God listens.

Compare these two passages. What ideas or words are repeated? In three words or less, what is the main theme of the passage from Psalm 116? What is the main theme of the passage in Psalm 118? What has the writer learned about God? What do these passages say about this writer's relationship to God? About his prayer life?

Martin Luther said, "Whoever prays the Psalms earnestly and regularly will soon stop those other light and personal little devotional prayers and say: Ah, there is not the juice, the strength, the passion, the fire which I find in the Psalms."

John Wesley said there is so much of Christ in the Psalms. They bring us into communion with God. Deitrich Bonhoeffer said the Psalms are the voice of Jesus showing us how to pray. They show us that prayer is not about getting all the "thee's" and "thou's" in the right place, but about being honest with God. The Psalms are our assurance that our conversations with God—even the most raw and real ones—are heard by Him.

The writer of the book of Revelation enforces this point in his picture of life around the throne of God. In Revelation 5:8, we are shown the company of spiritual beings surrounding the throne, worshipping God. In the midst of the praise and worship are a series of bowls made of pure gold. The text tells us these bowls collect the prayers of the people. When our prayers fall into these bowls, they mix with fire (a biblical image for the power of God) and become like incense that fills the air around God. God is always with us, God is always surrounded by our prayers, always aware of what is being prayed.

Think about that for a minute. You know how we sometimes say, "It doesn't feel like my prayers are going any further than the ceiling"? Well, according to what the prophet John saw in his revelation, that's simply not true. Those are feelings, not fact—much like the disciples' feelings as they weathered their storm.

Our prayers are precious, every one of them. Right now, they are being collected in golden bowls, mixing with the power of God and at the right time, God will tip those bowls and pour His power and our prayers over the earth.

He hears us. Do you believe that? God hears you. Even if you don't feel like anything is happening in the natural world when you pray, in the spiritual realm, in the presence of God, your prayers are collecting, and at the right time God will pour out His response.

Encounter

My heart has heard you say, "Come and talk with me."
And my heart responds, "LORD, I am coming."   *—Psalm 27:8 (NLT)*

GOD, come close. Come quickly! Open your ears—it's my voice you're hearing!
Treat my prayer as sweet incense rising; my raised hands are my evening prayers.
                    —Psalm 141:1–2 (THE MESSAGE)

Using Psalm 91 as your guide, write a prayer to God expressing your deepest needs, your most difficult battles, and your most heartfelt praise. Write in psalm-form, then offer this prayer to God, visualizing Him receiving it as fragrant incense.

WEEK 6: EXERCISE #3

Nothing is more exhilarating than flying through the air on a zip line, high above trees or a river. To reap the joy of that experience, though, requires jumping into thin air. And jumping requires absolute trust in the rope that attaches the harness to the wire. Until that vertical connection is secure, it would be crazy to take that leap.

In the same way, when our vertical relationship is secure (human to God), it is a lot easier to leap into healthy horizontal relationships (human to human). Our trust must be rooted in God in order for our horizontal relationships to be healthy. If we have not resolved within ourselves that God can be trusted—that He is good, He is for us, and He is just—we will struggle in every area of life.

Read Matthew 25:14–30.

Who are the main players in this story? What is going on, exactly? After reading through the story, summarize it in your own words.

This is a story about trust. On the one hand is a guy who probably hasn't always treated the people around him with a lot of love and compassion. On the other hand is a servant who probably doesn't have a great track record of trusting people. His fellow servants managed to think the best of their master, but he wasn't able to make decisions from a place of trust. He learned the hard way that a lack of trust can sabotage our relationships and opportunities.

When we enter into relationships from a place of suspicion rather than trust, we will struggle to make progress toward building healthy sustainable, enjoyable relationships. It begins with us.

In this story, with whom do you identify most? Why?

Imagine you are the lawyer in charge of trying the case between the unjust manager and his servant. Make a case arguing first in defense of the unjust manager, and then in defense of the servant.

Trust is one way to cultivate the soil of our spiritual life. Trust breaks up hard soil and creates a better environment for growth. The Lord wants us to continue to grow in our relationship with Him, and it requires trusting Him with our whole heart.

Look again at the story of the unjust manager and lazy servant. How could the servant have built trust in this relationship, rather than acting on his distrust? What one thing could you do right now to act on your trust in God, rather than on distrust or doubt? What practical acts of trust could you try out in your closest relationships? Pray into this, and pick three practical things you could do this week to intentionally build trust and break up the hard soil of a vertical or horizontal relationship.

Encounter

Trust in the LORD with all your heart and lean not on your own understanding;
in all your ways submit to him, and he will make your paths straight.

—Proverbs 3:5–6

Trust God. It sounds so simple, yet it is the most profound thing we do. In the wilderness of hard times, in hard or rocky soil, God desires even then to forge a relationship of trust.

Do you trust God? Can you turn to Him in your confusion, weariness, and pain, trusting He'll be there to hear you and that He cares? Journal on these questions.

Take a few moments now and turn toward God. Cry out to Him honestly with all your heart, believing He hears and trusting He will provide, even if you do not know what to ask for.

Read Romans 8:26. In this place of prayer, allow the Spirit of God to pray for you, voicing before God even the things you don't know how to ask for. Try to simply be in God's presence without words, trusting the Holy Spirit to speak for you in this moment.

WEEK 6: EXERCISE #4

You know the old saying: "Sometimes big things come in small packages." Both the parables and their subject matter in Luke 13:18–21 fit that saying. To drop a little seed into the soil of a big field doesn't seem like much of an accomplishment. To knead the dough required for a days' worth of bread is hardly worth talking about. A mustard seed and a little yeast. Small things. Surprising results.

By the time we read these little parables, Jesus has been traveling the countryside engaging in a countless series of small encounters with ordinary people. He has had conversations over meals. He has shared stories about God. He has gathered a few friends. Small things, surprising results.

Jesus knows what's ahead. From these seemingly insignificant encounters, the Kingdom of God is being planted into the earth. His followers will continue to work the message into every opportunity, until one day every knee bows and every tongue confesses that Jesus Christ is Lord.

Small beginnings. Big results.

Read Luke 13:18–19.

Jesus asks a question (underline it in your Bible). Then, before anyone can answer, He proceeds to share a lesson. He knows His hearers have an expectation of what it will be like when the Messiah comes to claim His Kingdom. They expect a king who will give them freedom. They are looking for a warrior who will defeat the Romans and restore Israel to its former glory. They expect a great takeover. But this is not how the Kingdom of

God is designed to work, so before anyone can utter a word, Jesus answers His own question.

This is how something small can have a great impact. It is planted quietly, like a seed. It is worked into the culture slowly, like a woman kneading bread. The mark of a Kingdom thing is not speed or great size. The mark of a Kingdom thing is that it grows.

Given that definition, where do you see the Kingdom at work in the garden of your life? Where do you see progress in your spiritual life, in your relationships, in your service to others? How is your life bearing fruit, however slowly, for the Kingdom of God?

Read Luke 13:20–21.

Again Jesus asks a question (underline this one too).

Whenever something is repeated in Scripture, it is worth noticing. Repetition is a way of emphasizing something important. Clearly, Jesus wants us to understand the Kingdom of God. When Jesus preached and taught, that was most often His subject. When He sent His followers out into surrounding villages, He charged them to drive out demons, cure disease, proclaim the Kingdom of God, and heal the sick (Luke 9:1).

Jesus wants us to understand the nature of God's Kingdom. But not only *understand* it. He wants the Kingdom of God to *invade* us, like a plant taking over a garden or yeast working through dough. Jesus wants the Kingdom of God to come to bear on our lives, to change us, to make our small lives significant!

Compare your life ten years ago with your life now. Whether or not you were a follower of Jesus ten years ago, your life has surely changed. Make some notes in your journal. How has knowing Jesus changed your life? Has it made a difference in the choices you make, the company you keep, the habits you've formed? As more and more of Jesus has gained access to more and more of you, what impact has the Kingdom of God made on the living of your life?

Encounter

A testimony is presentation of evidence in support of the truth. In Christian terms, a testimony is an opportunity to point to the truth of Jesus.

In the two parables we've just studied, Jesus has taught us that a lot can be said in just a few words. Our testimonies don't always have to be life stories. Sometimes they can be as simple as sharing how the presence of Jesus changed a situation, or changed our perspective. It can be as simple as saying, "Here's where I was in this situation. Here's what happened when Jesus showed up. Here's how it turned out." Learning to interpret life through the lens of encounters with Jesus can completely change our perspective and it can encourage others around us.

Take time now to jot down a few events in your journal that were impacted by the presence of Jesus. Maybe it was a time when . . .

- you witnessed the love of God in action and were amazed.
- you were obedient to an inner nudge to reach out to someone and it paid off.

- you were feeling spiritually dry, then encountered God's presence in a fresh way.
- you were encouraged by someone's comment when you were growing in your faith.
- someone showed up at just the right time with just the right words.

Journal one or more of these experiences, using the pattern mentioned above ("Here's where I was in this situation. Here's what happened when Jesus showed up. Here's how it turned out.").

Now pray for an opportunity to share the Kingdom of God and "plant" one of these seeds into someone's life as a way of encouraging them.

WEEK 6: EXERCISE #5

How many church people does it take to change a lightbulb?
Change?! What do you mean change? My grandmother gave that lightbulb!

For average church people, change can be a four-letter word. We like the thought of going somewhere spiritually but not if it requires us to get outside our comfort zones. And yet, the call of Christ is to come and die, to change, to be transformed. And transformational growth usually happens not in times of comfort and ease but when trials and temptations are the greatest.

Read Exodus 14.

As you read through this part of the story of the Israelites' deliverance from Egypt, ask the basic questions: Who? What? When? Where? Why?

Who are the main players in the story? What were they doing? What was their role in the story? Where were they? Why were they there?

The Israelites were a fickle people. They loved God, but often found themselves battling their own selfish desires and fears. When they found themselves at the edge of the Red Sea with an army at their back, they complained like crazy.

They said to Moses, "Was it because there were no graves in Egypt that you brought us to the desert to die? What have you done to us by bringing us out of Egypt? Didn't we say to you in Egypt, 'Leave us alone; let us serve the

Egyptians'? It would have been better for us to serve the Egyptians than to die in the desert!"

—Exodus 14:11–12

Over and over, they allowed doubt, fear, and pure selfishness to drive their responses to the challenges of life in the desert. And it was their poor responses (not God's bad directions!) that left them wandering in the wilderness for forty years.

Write the text of verses 13 and 14 in your journal. Take a few moments to meditate on these verses. What do you learn about God from these verses? What do you learn about the Israelites? What do you learn about God's relationship to the Israelites?

Life happens to all of us. As the Bible says, the rain falls on the just and the unjust alike. We don't get to choose all our circumstances, but we do get to choose how we respond to life. And how we respond probably says more about our relationship to God than most anything else.

What do your responses to life say about your relationship to God these days?

What do your prayers say about your relationship to God?

Read Galatians 5:16–26; Philippians 1:3–6; and Luke 1:37.

Paul teaches us that the fruit of the Spirit is love, joy, peace, patience, kindness, goodness, gentleness, faithfulness, and self-control. The first thing on that list is love. The primary mark of the Holy Spirit is a supernatural ability to love, and in fact to love so much that we are not offended by those around us but instead are driven to share the love of Christ with them. To be filled with the Holy Spirit is to be so filled with compassion that all we really want is the other person's joy.

For the Spirit-filled Christian, that's what it means to be fruitful. The real power of the Holy Spirit is love that works itself out in practical acts of witness and compassion.

Where in your life is the fruit of the Holy Spirit evident?

God's desire is to invade our lives, to transform us from the inside out. The goal is that we look less like the person we have been and more like the Christ we follow. It begins with a choice, and it results in the kind of fruit that gives witness to the Kingdom among us.

Encounter

But the fruit of the Spirit is love, joy, peace, patience, kindness, goodness, faithfulness, gentleness and self-control. Against such things there is no law.
—*Galatians 5:22–23*

In your journal, make a vertical list of the fruits listed above, with space between each word. This list is the foundation of this time of prayer and meditation. Focusing on one word at a time, ask Jesus to show you how you are displaying this character trait of a follower in your everyday life. "Lord, where is evidence of Your love shining through me?" As the Lord reveals situations to you, make notes beside the word.

Now, ask God to show you where in your life you are not displaying this trait of a follower. "Lord, where am I falling short of Your best when it comes to actively loving others?" Again, make notes.

As you move through the list of nine "fruit of the Spirit," continue asking questions like those above. Be intentional about noting both those places in your life you can celebrate as well as those places that need prayer and practice.

As you come to end of this meditation and prayer practice, thank God for grace!

WEEK 7: EXERCISE #1

Read Deuteronomy 5:1–22; Matthew 5:17–20; Mark 12:28–34; and Romans 6:14.

Read these Scriptures through the filter of the Spirit of Jesus. With each passage, ask, "What does this passage *say*? What does this passage *mean*? What does this passage mean *to me*?"

Now, create a large box on your journal page (big enough to make notes on the inside, but with room to write around the edges). Around the outside of the box (outside the lines that make the box), write a summary version of the Ten Commandments, as you find them listed in Deuteronomy 5:1–22. On the inside of the box, write what you hear Jesus saying about these commandments from the New Testament Scriptures you've just read.

Do any of the commandments or laws stand out for you as particularly relevant? Are there any that don't seem important to you? Why?

Consider your own faith journey in light of this graphic. What healthy boundaries are keeping you inside the pasture and under the care of Jesus? What boundaries have actually set you free? Are there places in your life where you tend to focus more on the fence than the pasture?

Encounter

Draw another large box. Around the outside, list the healthy, holy boundaries that are keeping you inside the pasture and under the care of Jesus. Maybe for you it is the decision to quit an addiction, or a more healthy approach to relationships. What are the holy habits that give structure and peace to your life?

Now, inside the box write those things you've discovered in following Jesus that make this journey more joyful, more meaningful, than what you used to know.

The essence of the Christian faith is placing confidence in the One sent by God. Does your life reflect that kind of confidence? Do you trust God with the details of your life? What areas of your life need to be bordered with a holy discipline? In what areas of your life do you need to focus more on grace and less on rules? Continue to make notes in and around your box as you reflect on these questions.

Looking at the graphic you've just made, would you say that the life you have now is better than the one you had before you encountered Jesus?

Talk honestly to Jesus about your discoveries. Give thanks for progress made.

WEEK 7: EXERCISE #2

In our fast-paced, noisy world, the thought of being quiet and listening almost seems like an impossible task. Remember that Psalm 46:10 says, "Be still, and know that I am God."

Being still is an act of trust. It means trusting that He's on the receiving end of this moment, and it means *trusting God with everything I won't accomplish while I'm in that quiet place*. It means trusting that He loves me, and won't condemn me if I fall asleep while I'm still.

What do we get out of stillness? In the quiet place, we encounter not only the holiness of God but the truth of our own brokenness and sin. It is a willingness to lay myself out there before God, and to let Him do the hard but good work of sanctification in my life.

Read Luke 11:1–13.

What do you observe concerning the desire of the disciples?

Make a list of "teaching points" Jesus gives on the subject of prayer.

What one thing do you learn about prayer from this reading? Or what one thing are you remembering again? What promises does Jesus mention?

Read Mark 9:2–7.

What is God's command at the end of this scene?

What do you think God meant when He asked His disciples to "listen to [Jesus]"?

Is listening part of your prayer journey? What keeps you from the listening side of prayer? How would your prayer life change if you were to make an intentional effort to listen as much as you speak?

Encounter

Learning to hear the voice of God is a discipline that takes time and practice. In a past encounter, you were asked to spend a few minutes in quiet, listening for God. This time, let's try extending that time so that you're sitting quietly for fifteen minutes. Spend the time with pen in hand, listening for the voice of Jesus. Devote at least fifteen minutes to being present to God, still (but not asleep!), listening and journaling what you hear.

Trust what you hear in that place of prayer and write it down, believing God has both the power and the desire to speak into our lives. This is God praying through us, and this is how most of the Bible was written. It was written by faithful people who wrote while they listened.

Close your prayer time by reflecting on one verse from the following options: Psalm 23; Numbers 27:16–17; Isaiah 53:6.

WEEK 7: EXERCISE #3

Before moving forward with this exercise, review your journal notes from week three, during which we studied John 9. In the lessons of that week, we talked about how Jesus transforms our hearts and lives. John 9 provides the "backstory" for the chapter we are about to study.

Read John 10.

The story of the Good Shepherd in John 10 begins with the blindness of the Pharisees. Spiritual blindness seems to characterize the whole community, and especially the spiritual leadership.

Darkness in the spiritual life is not always a bad thing. St. John of the Cross (1542–1591) in *Dark Night of the Soul* talked about a season in the life of any serious follower of Jesus that feels very much like a "wall" to a runner. Some people call this a crisis of faith. It is a place on the spiritual journey where we have to consciously decide to choose Jesus in areas of our life we haven't given to Him yet. On the other side of a dark night, we experience a deeper hunger for God than we've known before.

God may sometimes walk us through a valley or a dark night. The enemy uses darkness too. Job mentions thieves and evildoers who hide in the dark.

Dr. Timothy Laniak writes:

One of the many words Job uses for darkness is tsalmavet, *found ten times throughout the book. This graphic compound term can be translated "shadow of death" or "deadly darkness." We're familiar with the phrase in The Shepherd Psalm: "Even though I walk through the valley of the shadow of death, I will fear no evil, for you are with me." Here the psalmist is unafraid to walk through the valley of* tsalmavet *because the Lord accompanies him. This valley symbolizes life's hazardous transitions—occasions when the Shepherd Guide could be trusted without the illumination of daylight.*[7]

In Isaiah 9:2 we are promised that the people who walk in darkness will see a great light and that the light will shine on those who live in death's shadow. There is great hope in that promise. If we are experiencing a time of spiritual confusion or a "dark night of the soul," the Light will eventually come. He will not leave us in the dark.

Read Luke 22:53; Luke 23:44–46; 1 Thessalonians 5:5; and Job 12:22.

How would you describe the darkness in each of these Scriptures?

What gives you hope in the darkness? Have you experienced a crisis of faith, or a "dark night of the soul"? What truth or grace carried you through that time?

What story from Scripture speaks most deeply in your dark times?

Encounter

Blessed are those who hunger and thirst for righteousness,
for they will be filled.

—Matthew 5:6

Times of trial and sacrifice are often paths to a greater hunger for God. Spiritual disciplines like fasting also create a great hunger for God.

Fasting is a prime opportunity to build trust in God, and it is a normal part of what it means to follow Jesus. Fasting is a biblical principle. There is nothing like it to break strongholds and release spiritual power into our lives.

Fasting is a way we can live what Jesus taught. It creates humility in us, which is a defining character trait of Jesus. And it gets our hearts ready for the next thing God has for us. Fasting makes us hungry to *live this*.

If your physical health allows, pick a meal—preferably today—and fast from eating for that meal. Spend the time instead roaming through your Bible looking for passages on hunger. Journal what you find. Then spend some time meditating on Matthew 5:6. Do you hunger and thirst for God? Close in prayer, asking God to give you a greater hunger for the things of His Kingdom.

WEEK 7: EXERCISE #4

As a child, were you a climber? Some of us loved the challenge of a sturdy tree, a tall fence, or a concrete ledge. We'd rather climb over a thing than go around it. But as adults, most of us would rather find the gate than climb the fence. When Jesus calls Himself "the gate," He's appealing to the adult in us who understands there is a hard way to get things done and an easy way. To enter into relationship with Jesus is to take the better option.

Read John 10:1–6.

After leaving his sheep in a safe place for the night, the shepherd now comes to the gate to lead them out. Since there are other flocks gathered there in the same pen, the shepherd calls to his sheep so they'll hear his voice. The relationship between sheep and shepherd is intimate. The shepherd knows his sheep. Sheep know to whom they belong. The shepherd cares for them and keeps illness and enemy at bay.

The average life span of a sheep is ten to twelve years. Over that time, consider how often the shepherd counts, checks, carries, nurses back to health, rescues, protects, feeds, shears, leads, and calls out to his sheep. No wonder they are considered part of the family.

A troubled lamb—one struggling to get along in the flock—would be relegated to the shepherd's shoulder, where it would be carried and talked to for long stretches of time. The point was for the lamb to learn the shepherd's voice.

Read Psalm 23.

The usual place of a shepherd is behind or beside his flock. But in the wilderness and unfamiliar territory, sheep need guidance and strong leadership to feel safe. In those situations, the shepherd is *out front* leading his flock.

In the same way, when we don't feel secure we do not feel free to function in the way God intended. Without walls, we lose direction, unity, and hope. Without walls, we tend to fade into the world around us.

How well do you know the voice of your Shepherd? Are you allowing Him to lead, guide, and direct you? How is your life influenced by the knowledge that you are known, protected, and cared for?

Do you see a link between spiritual blindness (John 9) and the shepherds and sheep (John 10)? What comparisons can you draw?

What contrasts do you see between the religious leaders in chapter 9 and the shepherd in chapter 10?

Read John 10:7–18.

Write down all the promises you find in these verses.

What do you notice about the thieves and robbers?

Thieves and robbers climb fences, motivated by greed and deception. Their plans are foiled when the sheep don't listen. In your life, what (or who) has come to steal, kill, or destroy your peace, faith, joy, obedience?

Jesus came to give us life and life to the full, abundantly, beyond measure (John 10:10; Psalm 23:5). Jesus gives. Thieves take. What things in your life have given you joy and abundance? What things (even those that sounded like a good deal on the front end) have stolen your joy? What have you learned from those experiences?

Encounter

There are good shepherds and bad shepherds. Jesus is a *good* shepherd. A good shepherd knows His sheep by name and is willing to lay down His life for the sheep. The sheep only have to listen to the voice of the shepherd. In other words, it is not about us. It is about the shepherd.

Close your eyes. Take a few deep breaths. Visualize Jesus standing before you. What do you know about Him? Make a list of everything you know to be true about Jesus, and everything you are experiencing even now as He stands before you. Who is this Jesus and how is He changing your life?

Google the hymn "Be Thou My Vision," and either print out the lyrics or listen to it online. Make this beautiful song into a prayer to the God of your life.

WEEK 7: EXERCISE #5

Read John 10:14–18 and 1 John 4:16–18.

As you read these Scriptures, focus on why the Father loves Jesus. Underline or highlight the relevant words and phrases in your Bible. What phrase in these Scriptures captures your attention? What do you learn from these verses about the connection between love and sacrifice?

Reread John 10:17.

In this verse, Jesus reveals the profound nature of His relationship with the Father. It is a relationship built on sacrifice, love, and hope. Jesus lays down His life in obedience to the Father's will. The Father loves Jesus. The hope is in the promise of overcoming death.

There is a "holy flow" of love and obedience present in a right relationship with God. The sheep follow the shepherd. The shepherd does everything in obedience to the Father. The Father loves the shepherd and the sheep.

As love and obedience flow through our relationship with God, we are made holy and we begin to experience the abundant life promised by Jesus. What happens when we stifle that "holy flow"?

Have you had the experience of being lured in by a project or idea that you knew was beyond God's cover? How did that work out for you?

Read Psalm 139.

David tells us that God knows us and that this is the foundation of our trust in Him. At the end of Psalm 139, David prays maybe the deepest prayer of trust. He opens every door of his heart and invites God in. "Search me, God, and know my heart; test me and know my anxious thoughts. See if there is any offensive way in me, and lead me in the way everlasting" (Ps. 139:23–24).

What does it mean to draw close to God? It is about moving past a belief in God to an experience of God. He is not disgusted by our doubts or frustrated by our fears. He is not angry about our immaturity or afraid of our pain. God in His ultimate wisdom and love has chosen to know us fully. No shame. No rejection. The cross is our assurance of that.

Encounter

We are going to use Psalm 23 as a foundation for our prayer time.

First, read through this psalm in two or three translations. You can find multiple translations online at www.biblegateway.com.

Choose a translation that feels comfortable to you and read the psalm again, making it into a prayer. Use first-person language. Make it your own prayer to God.

Now, pray the prayer again, adding as many specifics into the language as you can. For instance, rather than simply saying, "The Lord is my shepherd, I shall not want," we pray instead, "The Lord is my shepherd, I shall not want for my mortgage payment, my tuition, my car repair . . . "

Continue through the psalm, customizing it to your life. Journal as you go, making notes about how this psalm speaks into your deepest needs.

How does this method of prayer—using a psalm as a foundation—strengthen your understanding of God's plan for your life? How does it help your awareness of who Jesus is for you?

WEEK 8: EXERCISE #1

One of the most read books of all times begins with this line: "It is not about you."[8]

Absorbing that truth is the first step to encountering Jesus. Until we get it—really get it—that this life is about Jesus, we will miss out on the greatest treasures life has to offer.

Read Acts 9:1–19; Genesis 32.

In these passages, where do you see signs of self-centeredness? What about signs of surrender? Make notes in the margins. Underline words and phrases that stand out. What do you learn from the main players in these two stories about going with God?

Read Matthew 10:38–39.

We often hear someone say, when they are talking about a difficult part of their life, "I guess that's my cross to bear." Usually, we are talking about something we dislike dealing with. What do you think Jesus means when He says, "If you refuse to take up your cross and follow me, you are not worthy of being mine"(NLT)? Why would Jesus say we're not worthy of Him unless we identify with His cross?

What does Jesus mean when He talks about "clinging to your life"? What does that look like in practical terms?

What are you clinging to that might cause you to lose your physical life? Your spiritual life?

How would you describe a life totally committed to Christ? Is that a life you're interested in living?

Encounter

Read James 4:7–10.

As you read this testimony, reflect on your own understanding of repentance and grace.

> I spent my church life being told to repent, but I was an adult before I knew that repent meant (or at least involved) change. I was taught that "the middle of SIN is 'I'!" but not necessarily to forgive. I was taught about the new life in Christ, but I always saw it as a goal to reach, not a gift of salvation. I have never enjoyed repentance but endured conviction which led not to freedom but self-hatred. Now I know that confession without change really isn't repentance; it's just guilt. I am very grateful that God is now showing me the softer side of salvation—the freedom of the gift. Conviction is not the end but the beginning. And repentance is the completion of a beautiful process of cleansing.
>
> I've spent my whole life asking myself, "Why would anyone ever want to be a Christian?" For the first time ever, I know. It's not because it feels good, but because it is good.

Journal a response to this testimony from your own experience. Then write in your own words what repentance means to you. Spend some time in conversation with God, asking Him to show you where in your life you have yet to complete that process of repentance.

WEEK 8: EXERCISE #2

Read Numbers 13–14; Jeremiah 29:11–14.

Ten men became afraid and doubted the promises of God. Because of their fear they persuaded a whole community into disobedience. Their influence caused great distress for the people of God. However, two men dared to believe in the Mountain Mover, the One who held the future. They chose to follow totally after God, in whom they placed complete trust.

On what truths did Joshua and Caleb base their commitment? Make a list of those truths.

Do you have a vision for going someplace spiritually? Do you sense God leading you into the future? How are you drawing near and abiding in Jesus as you continue to trust Him with your future?

Encounter

God wants to bless us. This is written into the Scriptures from beginning to end. God is a blessing God and we are a blessing people. When our lives line up with His purposes, we come under the blessing and experience the abundant life.

The Bible is full of blessings. Take some time to read through these: Numbers 6:24–26; Psalm 121:7–8; Romans 15:13.

Choose one that speaks into your life and write it on an index card that you can tape to your computer or car dash.

Who in your life could use your blessing today? How could you use one of these Scriptures to pour a blessing over someone, either in prayer or by some practical act of kindness?

WEEK 8: EXERCISE #3

Read Ephesians 3:14–21.

As you read, underline all the phrases describing God. Circle the phrases and words that indicate Paul's heart for people.

In one of the most powerful and heartfelt prayers of the New Testament, Paul prays for all believers to be strengthened through the power of the Holy Spirit in our relationship with Jesus. Paul longs to see followers of Jesus wildly abandoned to the ideals of the Kingdom of God. He yearns for us to be rooted and established in love and to grasp the remarkable, lavish love of Christ.

Such a prayer deserves our attention. Take a moment to rest in the knowledge that this prayer of Paul was prayed over *you* . . . nearly 2,000 years ago. This is the prayer of a righteous man who deeply cared about your life in Christ.

Let's look at some of the key terms in this prayer. Paul prayed that we might be rooted and established in love. To be rooted is to have a firm footing, to be entrenched. Being rooted in Christ is not the same thing as assenting to a set of beliefs. It is about planting our lives in the soil of Jesus, drawing our spiritual food from Him.

There is a beautiful benediction in this prayer. Paul says, "Now to Him who is able to do far more abundantly all that we ask or think . . . " (NASB). The NIV Bible uses the phrase, "immeasurably more."

God's idea of "big" is a lot bigger than ours. And God intends at the end of His work to receive all glory for it.

Paul's prayer gives us a powerful tool for praying over those we love. Write this prayer on an index card and put it in your Bible. Personalize it and use it to pray over the lives of your children, your spouse, and your church.

Encounter

Plant the good seeds of righteousness and you will harvest a crop of love.

—*Hosea 10:12 (NLT)*

Read Galatians 6:7–10.

Paul sowed into countless lives, and not just those he personally encountered. Through his writings and prayers, he continues to sow into lives today.

The principle of sowing and reaping says that what we plant will bear fruit. Paul says, "You will always reap what you sow."

How can you share the love of Jesus this week with someone, planting seeds of righteousness through practical acts of kindness? Who in your life needs a note or some other expression of care? What prayers are you sowing into the lives of the people you love?

Make a list in your journal of those you'd like to sow into spiritually, and begin now to pray for them.

WEEK 8: EXERCISE #4

John 13–17 describes Jesus' last hours with His disciples. He washes their feet, shares a final Passover meal, and reveals that He is about to be betrayed. Sensing their troubled spirits, Jesus promises He will give them the Holy Spirit to be a comfort and help to them. They will not be left alone. God will be with them. He then tells His disciples as John 14 closes, "Come now; let us leave" (John 14:31).

When the meal is over, Jesus takes the disciples on a two-mile walk out of the city to the Garden of Gethsemane. Can you imagine the spiritual and emotional heaviness these followers felt as they made that walk together? Passing through vineyards as they traveled, Jesus offered one more picture of who He really was.

Read John 15:1–11.

"I am the true vine, and my Father is the gardener." The image of the vine was a familiar image in Jewish culture and history. A vine was engraved on Jewish coins. It decorated the front of the Holy Place in the Temple. Their Scriptures (our Old Testament) described Israel as God's vine or vineyard (Isa. 5:1–7; Jer. 2:21; Ezek. 15; and Ps. 80:8–9). The grapevine was a symbol of hope for the Jewish people.

Now Jesus gives the grapevine a whole new meaning. "I am the vine." It is Jesus who will produce the fruit of hope. It is Jesus who is over the temple and over Israel itself.

The Greek word *airo* means to lift up or take away. In the dry season, root systems easily become disconnected from the main vine, the source of their nutrition. To keep the system healthy, some roots have to be lifted up or pruned. The gardener's job is to carefully tend these systems, lifting (or pruning) root systems that have become disconnected.

Hearing Jesus' teaching in *this* light makes it all the more powerful when we apply it to our own spiritual lives. This is a word about the hard work of letting go of those things that draw energy away from our growth in Jesus.

What in your life is sapping you spiritually? What dead roots need to be lifted up, examined honestly, and pruned?

In a Jewish vineyard, stones mattered. Branches resting on a stone didn't develop separate root systems, but remained fully connected to the main vine, allowing the vine to do its work in producing the fruit. Our focus should be on staying connected to Jesus. Abiding in Him. Obeying Him. Keeping His commands.

So where is your focus these days? Are you abiding? Are you able to simply "be" with Jesus? Is this a point that needs repentance and prayer?

Read John 15:12–17.

Jesus is clearly pouring everything He has into these dear followers as they make their way to the place where He would be betrayed.

He tells them about the power of praying in His name. He gives them a new command, to love one another. He calls them to a life of abiding, to an intimate connection with the Vine.

Jesus wants His followers to become like Him: to love as He loves, to give as He gives, to forgive as He forgives, to pray as He prays. And then, He calls these followers His friends *not* because of what they do but because of *who they are*. They have been faithful to Him, and He will now be faithful to them, even to the end.

What kind of relationship did these disciples have with Jesus? What kind of relationship do you have with Jesus? Have you accepted the reality that Jesus loves you and accepts you as His friend?

Jesus wants to meet with you face to face. He chooses you. Will you choose Him?

Encounter

Reaching out to love one another is not always an easy thing to do. In order to love as Jesus intends, we must remain connected to Him.

Make a list in your journal of at least three people in your life:
1. One who is easy to love.
2. One who is difficult to love.
3. One who is unlovable in your eyes.

Next to the each person's name begin to write the following questions and statements:
- To whom can I show favor for the Father's sake?
- How can I show kindness?

- What one good quality do I see in this person?
- How can I pray God's best over this person?
- How is Jesus asking me to bear fruit in this person's life?

As you pray through your list, listen for promptings of the Holy Spirit. Remember the mark of the Holy Spirit is a supernatural ability to love. When we are obedient to the commands of Jesus, even when we don't feel like it, we surrender our own ways and open the door for an authentic encounter.

WEEK 8: EXERCISE #5

Read John 13.

In John 13, the story is told of Judas, the most notorious rebel in the Bible. Just before Jesus is arrested, all the disciples are there at the table with Jesus. John tells us that "the one whom Jesus loved" was sitting right next to Jesus on one side. Most folks assume that person was John himself. If so, notice that John does not see himself primarily as a follower or an apostle or as a certain kind of disciple, but as "the one Jesus loved."

Most folks assume Judas was sitting on the other side of Jesus. So on one side sat John, the one Jesus loved. On the other side, Judas, the one who thought he needed to make it all happen on his own strength. On one side, John, who was leaning on grace; and on the other side, Judas, who lost confidence in grace.

Steve Harper, former president of Asbury Seminary's Orlando campus, says that spiritual dryness often begins right there, with a loss of confidence in God's grace. Spiritual dryness often grows in a theology "rooted in performance, whose voice keeps trying to convince us, 'You are worth only as much as you do; valuable only as long as you produce; in My will only as you succeed.'" And out of that mindset comes great workers and even great churchgoers. But not great faith.

So there at the Last Supper, on the two sides of Jesus, are the two kinds of *us*: grace and performance; the one Jesus loves and the one who wants control.

The question is: In this scene, which one are you? That's where it begins, really. With taking honest stock of how we see ourselves as spiritual beings. What if, from this day forward, you were to see yourself as the one Jesus loves?

Set your book down now, and speak this great truth into the spiritual realm: "I am God's Beloved."

What if you began to follow Jesus out of that motivation? Not because He was a great teacher or prophet or leader of people (though He was), but because He is the very love of God poured out you and over the whole world.

Jesus loves *you*. That's the great news of the red letters in the Bible.

The Jesus loves you.

That's a promise.

Encounter

Read John 17.

Before He left earth Jesus looked up to heaven, the Scripture says, and He prayed for you. He prayed a real prayer that you might be just as close to God as He was. He prayed that you would *know* He came from God and was sent here for your benefit. He prayed you would know God loves you every bit as much as He loved Jesus Himself. He prayed for the deeper knowing that comes through transformation. He prayed that when you and I encounter Jesus, we'd change.

And since Jesus is the same yesterday, today, and forever, then the prayer He prayed for us in the first century is the same prayer He is praying for us now as He continues to intercede for us at the right hand of the Father.

We are people for whom Jesus prays! Jesus Christ, Son of God, who lives and reigns with God forever, is praying for you. Jesus is praying for your faith, for your salvation, for transformation in your life. Jesus' great desire for you and me is that we have eternal life. And eternal life is ours when we know the one, true God and Jesus Christ, whom He sent.

The prayer Jesus prays for His followers in John 17 is one we can pray too. Praying Scripture is a great way to pray in agreement with God's will.

As we close this study, read John 17:20–23 and, in the spirit of the words of Jesus, pray this into your life:

> *Lord Jesus, I pray as one who believes in Your message. Make me one with the Father, just as You are in Him and He is in You. May I also be in Christ so that the world may believe in the One the Father has sent. Be glorified through my life and make me one with those You've called into the Body of Christ. Then the world will know that You are God's Son. I make this prayer in the name of Jesus, the One who changes everything. Amen.*

NOTES

Week 3, Exercise #2

1. Billy Graham, *Crusader Hymns and Hymn Stories* (Charlotte, NC: Billy Graham Evangelistic Assoc., 1965), 8.

Week 3, Exercise #4

2. Michael Card, *Parable of Joy* (Grand Rapids: Discovery House Publishers, 2007), 134.

3. W. E. Vine, Merrill F. Unger, William White, Jr., *Vine's Complete Expository Dictionary of Old and New Testament Words* (Nashville: Thomas Nelson, 1996), 556.

Week 5, Exercise #1

4. Message given at Willowcreek Leadership Summit, 2011

Week 5, Exercise #3

5. Janet Hagberg and Robert Guelich, *The Critical Journey: Stages in the Life of Faith* (Salem, WI: Sheffield Publishing Co., 2005).

Week 5, Exercise #4

6. Dr. Howard Vos, *Nelson's New Illustrated Bible Manners and Customs* (Nashville: Thomas Nelson, 1999), 460.

Week 7, Exercise #3

7. Dr. Timothy Laniak, *While Shepherds Watch Their Flocks: Reflections on Biblical Leadership* (Oviedo, FL: Higher Life Development Services, 2009).

Week 8, Exercise #1

8. Rick Warren, *The Purpose Driven Life*, rev. ed. (Grand Rapids: Zondervan, 2012), 23.